TEACHING
OUTSIDE
THE BOX

**Five Approaches
to Opening the Bible
With Youth**

ANDREW
ZIRSCHKY

TEACHING OUTSIDE THE BOX

Copyright © 2017 Andrew Zirschky

All rights reserved.

All Web addresses were correct and operational at the time of publication.

ISBN: 9781501823893

17 18 19 20 21 22 23 24 25 26—10 9 8 7 6 5 4 3 2 1

MANUFACTURED IN THE UNITED STATES OF AMERICA

CONTENTS

Table of Contents...3

Dedication 5

Acknowledgments..7

Preface..11

Introduction...15

Chapter 1: The Instructional Approach 35

Chapter 2: The Community of Faith Approach 57

Chapter 3: The Interpretive Approach 79

Chapter 4: The Liberation Approach 101

Chapter 5: The Contemplative Approach 131

Appendix: Leading Youth in Theological Reflection....................149

DEDICATION

For Dwight and Linde,

who brought me into this world

and together instilled in me a love for God,

a passion for teaching,

and a burning impulse to think outside the box.

ACKNOWLEDGMENTS

Some of the inspiration and design for this book arises from the work of Jack Seymour, who spent decades teaching religious education at Garrett-Evangelical Seminary and who devoted much of his written work to mapping and describing various approaches to Christian education. His influential 1982 book, *Contemporary Approaches to Christian Education* (written with Donald Miller) gave me a new framework for looking at Christian education that was useful even twenty-five years after its publication. Additionally, as I considered the approaches that Seymour and Miller delineated in that book, I realized that similar approaches were clearly operative in youth ministry down to the present time. In some ways this wasn't too much of a surprise given that youth ministry often operates as a subfield of Christian education. Nevertheless, I could immediately see the ways in which the various approaches described by Seymour and Miller found new contours in the context of youth ministry. I could also see that new approaches had been introduced directly to youth ministry since their book's release, and so I decided that modifying Seymour and Miller's framework and description of the approaches for youth ministry would be beneficial for youth ministers.

In 2010 I began teaching a course at Memphis Theological Seminary, "Communicating the Gospel to Youth," that introduced students to various approaches for teaching and forming teenagers in the faith; this book is a direct outgrowth of that course. Although I have never met Dr. Seymour, I am indebted to him. I've sought to recognize his influence by naming one of my main characters in his honor. That being said, all the characters in this book, including Seymour, are works of pure fiction and in no way are intended to represent real people, living or dead.

I would like to extend my appreciation to many people who have helped make this book possible: First, I need to thank former student and incredible youth worker, Tina Boyd, for her smart and diligent work on the curriculum examples that are referenced throughout the book. Tina was one of the best and brightest students I've had to date, and she worked magic to edit and revise (and in some cases create from scratch) the accompanying curriculum. Despite receiving virtually no guidance from me, Tina did a fantastic job and this book would have been impossible without her.

Second, I need to thank the dean and faculty of Memphis Theological Seminary (MTS) for graciously granting me a reduced teaching load in the spring of 2017, allowing me the time to write this book. MTS, through its partnership with the Center for Youth Ministry Training, boasts one of the largest, finest, and most exciting youth ministry programs in the country. It is an honor to be a contributing member of such a fine faculty. I'm especially thankful for my colleague in Christian education at MTS, Carmichael Crutchfield, who continues to sharpen my thinking about matters concerning the faith formation of adolescents.

Additionally, my colleagues at the Center for Youth Ministry Training patiently picked up my slack as I routinely disappeared from the office for writing time: Thank you Deech Kirk, Courtney

Hicks, Courtney Wilson, Deborah Livingston, Anna Kathryn Simmons, Corrie Summerville, Teresa Kingsbury, Kris Konsowitz, and Lesleigh Carmichael.

I also need to thank my children Evan and Anna who were patient during the "finish the book" time that in reality should have been theirs. And to their mother, Kristina, who filled in for my many absences. Thank you.

A thank you to Kenda Creasy Dean is always in order since she has been so influential in forming my thinking and academic work related to youth ministry. It was Kenda who originally introduced me to *Contemporary Approaches to Christian Education* by way of sharing previous incarnations of syllabi for a course she teaches at Princeton Theological Seminary. I also need to thank Michael Novelli for engaging with me in discussion and thought around the various approaches outlined herein. Tim Baker deserves special recognition for patiently waiting for me to provide him with a manuscript to edit for nearly two years. In typical fashion, I dumped the manuscript on his doorstep with a ridiculously short window of time for editing. He nevertheless helped heal the broken pieces of the manuscript and performed miracles. The many flaws that remain are solely my own.

Finally, I need to thank the many students in the Master of Arts in Youth Ministry program at Memphis Seminary who have learned (and suffered) through the course "Communicating the Gospel to Youth" in 2010, 2012, 2014, and 2016. With each incarnation of the course I learned to better describe the ideas and approaches for teaching and learning that are included within this book. My students were fabulous in asking questions for clarification, pointing out places of apparent paradox, and generally helping me better outline the approaches presented in the pages that follow. Thank you for being teachers of your teacher.

PREFACE

Recently my daughter Anna asked me, "What kind of book are you writing?" It's about teaching teenagers I told her. She stared at me with an annoyed second-grade look, as if grown-ups are the densest creatures ever and I'd just proven it once again. "Duh, you told me that, but is it nonfiction, realistic fiction, or fantasy fiction?" she asked, displaying her recently acquired knowledge of literary genres.

Good question, I thought. Some people would certainly classify the act of successfully opening the Bible with teenagers as fantasy fiction. However, after more than two decades in youth ministry, I've had enough experiences of wonder and discovery with youth to know that seeing Scripture impact the faith lives of young people is no fantasy. Nevertheless, Anna's question was a good one.

"This book is nonfiction mixed with realistic fiction," I explained. Indeed, the book in your hands is a story that didn't happen—at least not quite in the way that it unfolds in these pages. However, the story teaches something true. Set amidst a fictionalized narrative, the pages ahead reveal the journey of Jeremy, a youth worker, who discovers five approaches to teaching the Bible that open up the lives of teenagers and give them new eyes and ears they can use to discover the meaning of Scripture.

To change our approach to teaching means to change the very goal and desired outcome of the teaching itself. In this book you will not find gimmicks or teaching methods that attempt to creatively communicate something old in a new way. There are plenty of books available on teaching methods for youth ministry, and I recommend you read some of them. This book looks deeper and seeks to expand the goals with which you approach teaching youth.

Despite the myriad of curriculum resources released annually by Christian publishers, almost all of them approach teaching from what can be called the instructional approach. Up to this point, you may not have had a name for the way you teach, but chances are you do the vast majority of your teaching using the instructional approach. The goal of this approach, as it is often described by curriculum writers, is to help students understand a small portion of Scripture and then help them apply it to their lives. This approach is used over and over and over again in most churches because it is replicated over and over and over again in most published curriculum and teaching resources. Even those youth workers who write their own curriculum tend to fall into the instructional approach because it's all they've ever experienced. When they think about teaching Scripture, they think in instructional categories.

Even with the addition of clever teaching methods—video, roleplay, learning stations, or crazy games—again and again we approach Scripture with the goal of helping teenagers understand and apply it. In fact, as you're reading this text you may be wondering what other options there could be! Well, there are definitely other options and as we learn to utilize these additional approaches in the pages ahead, we can expect Scripture to come alive in new ways not only for us but also for the teenagers we teach.

There is not one right way to approach teaching Scripture, and I won't be advocating a particular approach out of the five presented, but I firmly believe we have to step outside our usual ways and limited approaches. We have to get outside the box in order to cooperate well with the Holy Spirit, the One who moves and transforms the hearts, minds, and lives of teenagers. Put simply, our hope is to enhance our ability as youth workers to utilize multiple approaches.

Accompanying this book as a digital download are the actual curriculum pieces mentioned in the narrative. They will help you get a sense of what the various approaches look like in actual teaching moments. Regardless, handing you curriculum is not my goal. My hope is that you'll come away with new ways for thinking about the task of opening Scripture with teenagers—ways of seeing and imagining that will impact your actual teaching far more than any curriculum example ever could.

Each of the approaches introduced opens Scripture in new and unique ways and, in doing so, opens the hearts and lives of teenagers to be transformed by the Holy Spirit in new and unique ways. That journey of discovery is what this book is about, and I invite you to join Jeremy, the main character in our story, in discovering what it looks like to teach outside the box.

INTRODUCTION

Two years into his youth director gig at Oak Harbor Church, Jeremy Bevins was finally beginning to get the hang of things. Navigating life in an aging mainline congregation was night and day from navigating college life, and the first year had been a shock to his system. Oak Harbor wasn't exactly teeming with young adults, so he'd felt relationally isolated. In addition, his expectations for what he would be doing in youth ministry were decidedly different from the expectations of the congregants.

Looking back, year one had been a fight for survival. There even had been a few Sunday mornings when he was close to tears and wanted to disappear. On a particularly difficult Sunday, he had sat in the back pew during worship and pondered running out the door, leaving his ministry job behind and starting over doing something else. Though there were numerous other days he'd considered quitting during that first year, he was thankful he'd stuck with it.

Despite the temptation to leave, there was finally light at the end of the tunnel. Teenagers started showing up for what had been a dwindling "youth program." (Jeremy preferred the term *student ministry*, but that change was shot down when the teenagers said they preferred *youth ministry*.)

Whatever, Jeremy thought. The teenagers of Oak Harbor were just one aspect of the church that mystified Jeremy. *Everyone and everything here is so backward, so small, so frustrating.*

When he'd seen the job posting for Oak Harbor Church in rural Tennessee, he had envisioned a quaint, sophisticated town nestled against the cove of a large lake with sail boats and vacation rentals. Since he'd failed to research the location before arriving for his interview, he was surprised and disappointed to find that Oak Harbor Church wasn't near any water. The town wasn't even called Oak Harbor. The church simply was on a road called Oak Harbor Lane. Because it was one of only two significant roads in a farming community, that side of town became known as Oak Harbor.

Life in rural Tennessee was not what Jeremy had imagined. Regardless of the location, he'd been thrilled to land a youth ministry job right out of college and, though the salary wasn't posh, he could manage his living expenses, pay his student loans, and only occasionally depend on bank deposits from his parents.

At age 24 he'd gained the independence that only a few of his friends had experienced. Some of them were in grad school, still racking up debt. Others were selling their souls in meaningless jobs. Still others were living at home with their parents. He even knew of a few friends who'd managed to fail simultaneously at all three scenarios by racking up debt, working in fast food, and living in their parents' basement. *Poor unfortunate souls*, he thought. Oak Harbor offered Jeremy the opportunity to actually design and build the student ministry—er, youth ministry—he'd dreamed of while maintaining some semblance of independence and adulthood.

As he eased into his second year at Oak Harbor, many aspects of the ministry were popping, with the notable exception of Sunday school. Jeremy desperately wanted to kill off this lumbering beast of a program that, in his opinion, had long outlived its usefulness. However, that conversation was a nonstarter.

He had been given permission to change the curriculum and format, but despite his best efforts nothing seemed to work. And lately parents (and youth) had been complaining that Sunday school was boring. Sunday school was the "same old stuff." The youth grumbled, "We've heard all this." And Jeremy grumbled about the same thing. He felt like he'd heard it all, too. So he changed the curriculum. He changed the curriculum again. Then, he found a video-based curriculum. It all flopped. It was almost as if the very hour was cursed, as if 10:00 Sunday morning had been declared by God as perpetually ineffective for teaching the Bible, or faith—or whatever it was he was supposed to be teaching. Frustrated in his attempts to "fix" Sunday school, Jeremy stopped exerting the effort. "They won't let me kill it, so I'll just let it die," he secretly plotted.

■ ■ ■ ■

Jeremy had just silenced the second snooze alarm when his phone suddenly lit up again, buzzing and vibrating the bedside table and sending a jolt through his subconscious. He snatched the phone from the table and peered closely at it, trying to align his eyesight beyond the blur of interrupted sleep.

A shock of panic shot down his spine when he saw the sender's name: Pastor Jack, longtime senior pastor of Oak Harbor Church and the one to whom he reported. He quickly checked the time thinking somehow he'd overslept again. Last spring he'd gotten into the habit of rolling into the office at around 10:30 a.m., but Jack had quickly put the kibosh on his laziness and established a firm 9:00 arrival time unless he'd been at a youth function the previous night.

"Please drop by my office when you get here this morning," the text read in perfect grammar and punctuation. "I'd like to speak to you about some issues."

Oh, great. What now? Jeremy thought to himself, looking around for something to curse. Mentally he began leafing through the possible incidents that could have prompted this summons to the pastor's office first thing on a Monday morning. *My polo was untucked yesterday at worship—but I was wearing khakis instead of jeans—so those should cancel out each other.* He checked any misstep with his attire off the list of possible offenses. Throwing back the covers, he sauntered to the shower, turned the hot water full on, and then leaned against the counter waiting for it to kick in.

We didn't have a youth activity yesterday so I can check that off. Dang. Did I say something outrageous or offensive in Sunday school? He replayed the previous morning's class in his mind, searching for something that could have sent one of his hypersensitive home-school kids scurrying back to their parents. *There was hardly anyone there, and I don't remember poking at anybody or saying anything that could have offended anyone.* (Jeremy had been chastised numerous times for his sarcasm and penchant for colorful language that the more conservative members of his congregation found inappropriate.)

Jeremy hadn't grown up in church, and he hadn't exactly lived the quaint and quiet life that most of his youth group attendees did. Having bounced from foster home to foster home for most of grade school and into middle school, he'd learned language and ways of verbally protecting himself that were dramatically different from the expected patterns of ministerial staff. He hadn't stepped foot into a church until he was in eighth grade and was adopted by a church-going family. Going to church wasn't really by his own choice as a teen, and it still shocked him that he was working in a church doing *ministry*—a word he didn't even know a few years prior.

Nope? I don't think I said anything, but who knows, Jeremy thought. He often found himself surprised when his congregants were shocked by things he said. "Get a filter," a church board member had once told him angrily after a joke Jeremy made. *Get a sense of humor*, Jeremy had thought in response.

On his drive to the church Jeremy continued pondering—and worrying—about why he had been summoned to Jack's office. By the time he reached the church parking lot, he had concluded that most likely his visit had something to do with the church custodian who routinely ratted on Jeremy for spilled juice or ground-in donuts on the youth room floor. "Stanley. It's got to be Stanley," Jeremy mumbled to himself. "The stupid, overeager janitor thinks he runs the place."

. . . .

Jeremy knocked gingerly and Pastor Jack waved him through his office door without turning from his computer. "Let me just finish this e-mail, Jeremy. Take a seat," he offered. Jeremy plopped onto the couch in the corner and began eyeing the various trinkets Jack had collected during his years in ministry. Tribal masks from a stint as a missionary in Papua New Guinea caught his eye, as did an intricate wooden cross crafted for Jack by one of the oldest members of the congregation. The pastor finally closed his laptop and, before he'd even swung his chair around, Jeremy launched out in defense.

"Look, I know we could do a better job cleaning up, but Stanley complains about everything," Jeremy pleaded. Jack was perplexed for a moment, but then said, "This isn't about the youth room; though you are correct, you could do a better job cleaning up."

Jeremy breathed a small sigh of relief, before quickly sucking it back in as Jack continued: "I'm concerned about your Sunday school program and, frankly, I'm also concerned about the teaching that's happening in the youth ministry. You run great events, Jeremy, and the teens have a good time. But when it comes to the actual teaching—week in and week out—there are a lot of complaints."

Jeremy shot back defensively, "There are always going to be complaints about the way we do ministry. You taught me that!"

"I did teach you that," Jack replied patiently, "but let me finish and hear me out. There are a lot of complaints, but my primary concern isn't the complaints. My concern is the attitude you've taken toward teaching youth generally. It's no secret that you're letting the youth Sunday school wither on the vine."

"OK. Yes, that's true. Because it's NOT effective. It's a dead program, and I think putting our energy into Wednesday nights when youth actually show up makes more sense," countered Jeremy.

"But Jeremy, do you really think the wrong day and time are the reasons why Sunday school isn't working? As if just moving teaching to another day will be a fix-all? I think what's broken is your approach to teaching—not whether it happens on Wednesdays or Sundays or whether it happens in youth group, Sunday school, or small-group Bible studies."

At the mention of small-group Bible studies, Jeremy got excited. "Yes! I've been wanting to start some small-group Bible studies. I think they would definitely be a better way for students to interact."

"Jeremy, utilizing small groups is one *method* of teaching. But they're not the silver bullet. No *method* is. What you need, I think, is to understand various *approaches* to opening up the Bible with youth and then be able to use them," offered Jack.

Jeremy wasn't quite following Jack's train of thought. He was trying to process the difference between method and approach, but he was coming up short.

Jack took advantage of the momentary silence and said: "So, here's what I want you to do. I want you to meet with an older member of our congregation. You probably don't know him because he doesn't leave the nursing home much these days, but I think you'd learn a lot from him. Before retiring he taught Christian education at a seminary in the city. When he moved here, he led the Sunday school program for quite a few years—and very successfully."

Jack paused, waiting for Jeremy to respond. But Jeremy was too shocked and just stared blankly, trying to take in what he'd just heard. Nursing home. Retired. Seminary. Christian education—whatever that meant. This was Jack's answer to issues with a Sunday morning class for teenagers?

"So his name," Jack said, breaking the awkward silence, "is Seymour Mathetai, and I'd like you to meet …"

Interrupting, Jeremy chuckled aloud and said, "His name is Seymour? Seriously, who does that to their child?" He immediately realized Jack wasn't the least bit amused at his reaction. "Sorry," he muttered sheepishly. (But the truth was Jeremy couldn't imagine a nursing home patient had anything to teach him about youth ministry—and he was even more skeptical now that the name Seymour had been revealed.)

"Jack, I really don't have the time to meet with him," Jeremy pleaded, looking for any excuse he could find to escape both this ridiculous discussion with Jack and a meeting with Seymour. "We have fall retreat coming up and students just started back to school, so we're working hard to get our Wednesday evening program running smoothly." Instead of responding, Jack pulled open a desk drawer and began rifling through it.

I thought Jack had more sense than this, Jeremy pondered as he waited for Jack to find whatever he was looking for. He was disappointed that someone he considered a mentor could be so thoroughly out of touch. Jeremy began to think that Jack seriously had no idea about what it takes to teach Scripture to twenty-first-century teenagers. His mind continued to rebel: *I thought he had a clue having worked with youth in the past, but how in the world was he successful in youth ministry when he thinks meeting with an octogenarian is the key to reviving my teaching ministry?*

Finally, Jack broke the silence as he pulled a fading church directory from the drawer and said, "I'm going to give him a call."

"Jack, seriously, I don't have time for this," Jeremy protested. "Fall retreat and …"

"You can make time for this, and I think it will be worth your time," countered Jack. "If nothing else it's worth the church's time for someone to call on Seymour. Maybe you'll learn something about the art of pastoral visitation as well as a few things about teaching. I could be wrong about the teaching thing, but I do know that Seymour is a wealth of information and was incredibly successful for years teaching teenagers in this church. I realize times have changed, but I'm going to bet there's at least a nugget or two you can gain from Seymour."

Times have changed, Jack. Times have certainly changed, Jeremy thought belligerently as Jack dialed. *But whatever.* He sat in silent protest as someone answered on the other end and Jack spoke. The conversation faded into background noise as Jeremy racked his brain for ways he could have avoided this visit to Old Man Detention with Seymour. *Maybe I should be playing more games or have a better opening?* he thought. He played out the scenarios in his mind. *I guess that would help some but, then again, I hardly have time to accomplish anything in Sunday school as it is. Wasting more time on games seems counterproductive. And it still doesn't address the fact that I have a bunch of middle school students who are telling me they've heard it all before.* "Arggh!" Jeremy audibly grunted to himself out of frustration with his students and with the fact that Jack was getting off the phone having arranged a meeting for him with Seymour.

"You're all set for 2 p.m. today," Jack smiled and said.

"Yep, OK," Jeremy muttered as he left the office. He didn't know what to feel. Anger? Righteous indignation? Or maybe just exasperation at being caught in a system that valued pastoral visits to old men when he had more than enough youth ministry responsibility on his plate.

I came to this church to minister to the next generation, not babysit the last, he thought selfishly. His thoughts devolved a bit further before he caught himself in a mental death spiral. *OK*, Jeremy thought, *get a grip. One meeting. In and out. You'll have done what Jack wants, you'll be able to cross Seymour off the visitation list, and then you can get back to your regularly scheduled student ministry job.* Then aloud he said, "One meeting!"

. . . .

A sign with 1980's styling and a hint of peeling paint announced Oak Harbor Assisted Living as Jeremy pulled into the parking lot. After inquiring at the front desk, Jeremy was asked to wait a moment before a middle-aged nurse named Jennifer arrived to escort him to Seymour's room. She led Jeremy down a long hallway with bright but aging floral wallpaper, and he noticed there were silk flower arrangements spaced along the way. The wooden chair rail along the length of the hallway made him think that it might just be the first time he'd actually seen something made of oak in Oak Harbor.

Welcome mats, pictures, crafts, and memorabilia adorned many of the residents' doorways, and he could hear televisions blaring game shows and talk shows as they passed the rooms. Jeremy was surprised to find the facility felt more comfortable than the hospital atmosphere he had imagined. *It's more like a college dormitory for old people*, he thought as they drew near to room 231.

Nurse Jennifer turned to him and said: "Here you are, Dear. This is Mr. Mathetai's room. I know he's up because I just checked on him a while ago. It seems he's having a very good day—or he was. You never know. Things do change," she commented with a hesitant tone. And with that she knocked firmly on the door and stepped aside. A second passed and Jeremy turned his ear toward the door, listening for a faint voice to tell him to enter.

He nearly jumped as the door came flying open. He was greeted by a spry man with a shock of gray hair, wearing a cable-knit sweater and thick glasses, while carrying a hefty mug of coffee. "Jeremy, come in! We have much to talk about," shouted Seymour in an excited tone, motioning for Jeremy to enter and spilling his coffee a bit in the process. "Ah …, take a seat, Jeremy. I need to clean up my mess. Getting clumsy with age. Oh, and thank you, Miranda," he said turning to the nurse.

"It's Jennifer, actually," she said patiently.

"Oh, yes. Well, thank you the same," he said as he shut the door swiftly, not at all concerned that he'd botched her name. Seymour rushed off to the kitchen at a faster pace than Jeremy had imagined a person of his age could and reappeared in seconds with paper towels, gesturing for Jeremy to follow him into the living room.

The efficiency apartment was small but clean and cozy. The walls were hung with fascinating pictures, art, and curios. Some sort of Australian aboriginal painting hung in one corner next to three intricately carved crosses. Beyond that the red and blue hues of a beautiful old page of an ancient Bible was framed. Jeremy peered closely at several other framed pictures of a younger Seymour traveling the world and posing with friends and acquaintances. Jeremy continued scanning the room as Seymour launched into conversation. "So I understand you're having some trouble teaching youth over at the church," Seymour said. "Pastor Jack said you're trying hard, but things just don't seem to be working?"

"Pretty much," Jeremy said, still scanning the walls. "You know, they've heard it all before, they're bored—and on it goes."

"*Yada, yada, yada*," interrupted Seymour, "that's the way it always is."

"Yoda?" Jeremy asked, looking puzzled.

"Oh. No, sorry," Seymour said with a chuckle. "*Yada*. It's Hebrew. It means 'I know'—same old, same old. Seymour laughed out loud at his attempted joke, spilling his coffee again. "Well, of course there wasn't Sunday school then, but teaching the Scriptures has always been a challenge," Seymour continued in a more serious tone. "So tell me what you've been doing lately. What approach are you taking?"

"Well, we've tried a lot of different curriculum, and we've reformatted the groups a few times. We tried taking them through a book of the Bible at first, but that bombed. We've tried meeting with guys and girls separately, and we've tried middle school and high school separately. Recently, we've been using a video curriculum. That seemed to hold their attention for a while, but not for long."

"Nah, nah, nah," Seymour interrupted, visibly annoyed. "I asked about your approach, and you're telling me about groups and video curriculum. Not what I'm interested in. Let me ask it this way: When you teach," he looked directly at Jeremy, "what do you believe the Holy Spirit is doing?"

Jeremy hadn't thought much about this before, and all that immediately came to mind was simply, *stuff*. Jeremy knew the Holy Spirit was doing something, but as he thought about Seymour's question, it didn't even make sense. "Well, I definitely believe the Holy Spirit is at work, but I'm not exactly sure what the Spirit is doing—I mean, who can know the ways of God, right?" Jeremy hoped that using a quasi-biblical phrase would score him some points. "I mean, we don't control the Holy Spirit. I'm really more focused on figuring out how to teach."

"Hmm. All true," Seymour said thoughtfully. Jeremy glanced at his phone to check the time, hoping this meeting would be over soon.

"But ...," Seymour let the word hang in the air for a moment and then, in a voice almost like a whisper, said, "How can you know what you should do as a teacher if you have no idea what God is doing and how you can cooperate with the Spirit?" The words gripped Jeremy, and he realized he'd never thought of this or anything like it. Jeremy silently mulled over the phrase, "cooperate with the Spirit," before Seymour continued.

"Your role in teaching Scripture, Jeremy, isn't to figure out how to make transformative learning happen," Seymour continued. "You are not the one who gives birth to faith, nor the one who enlivens the soul. You are not the one who makes Scripture come alive in the hearts and minds of young people. That is all the work of the Holy Spirit. Your job is not to teach but to figure out how to cooperate with the One who *is* The Teacher. What we call teaching in the church is actually a matter of trying our best to open up students to the work of the Holy Spirit. We have to be able to answer the question I just asked you." Seymour paused, letting each word hang in the air as he asked again: "What ... do ... YOU ... believe ... the ... Holy ... Spirit ... might ... be ... doing?"

Jeremy was both intrigued and terrified. He had no idea how to answer that question, though he knew he *should* know. *The Holy Spirit does something*, he thought, *but I have no idea what—and who am I to even guess?* Suddenly Jeremy heard the ticktock of a grandfather clock in the corner that he hadn't noticed before.

After a few moments, Seymour interrupted the silence and said: "I think you may have fallen into a very common trap, Jeremy. You see, if we don't have any idea what The Teacher might be doing, or any confidence that God will act, then we will flail around trying to do things not out of conviction but out of rote. Or to say it another way: We will be doing the same old things all the time while thinking that our actions might be enough to raise the dead. Other times we might try to be creative, but without an understanding of how God might act, this doesn't get us very far. Our actions are meaningless unless they're connected somehow with God's actions." Seymour could see Jeremy's blank stare indicating that he wasn't quite following, so Seymour continued: "How about this? Let me tell you a story. It's a story you probably know: the story of Elijah and the prophets of Baal."

Jeremy had no idea where this was going, but he nodded in agreement and sunk back into the cushions of the couch as Seymour reached for his Bible. This meeting wasn't going to be over as quickly as he'd hoped.

ELIJAH AND THE PROPHETS OF BAAL

Seymour adjusted his thick glasses and sat back into his chair, thumbing through the first pages of his large-print Bible. "Ah, yes. First Kings," he declared. "Fifteen, sixteen, here it is—eighteen." He peered up at Jeremy, "So as the story unfolds beginning in verse 21, Elijah is pitted against 450 prophets of Baal in one of the most epic showdowns in history—a showdown for the religious loyalty of Israel. Elijah calls for all of Israel to gather at Mount Carmel and when they arrive he issues a challenge." Looking down and adjusting his glasses again, Seymour began to read:

> "How long will you hobble back and forth between two opinions? If the LORD is God, follow God. If Baal is God, follow Baal." The people gave no answer.

> Elijah said to the people, "I am the last of the LORD's prophets, but Baal's prophets number four hundred fifty. Give us two bulls. Let Baal's prophets choose one. Let them cut it apart and set it on the wood, but don't add fire. I'll

prepare the other bull, put it on the wood, but won't add fire. Then all of you will call on the name of your god, and I will call on the name of the LORD. The god who answers with fire—that's the real God!"

All the people answered, "That's an excellent idea."

So Elijah said to the prophets of Baal, "Choose one of these bulls. Prepare it first since there are so many of you. Call on the name of your god, but don't add fire."

So they took one of the bulls that had been brought to them. They prepared it and called on Baal's name from morning to midday. They said, "Great Baal, answer us!" But there was no sound or answer. They performed a hopping dance around the altar that had been set up.

Around noon, Elijah started making fun of them: "Shout louder! Certainly he's a god! Perhaps he is lost in thought or wandering or traveling somewhere. Or maybe he is asleep and must wake up!"

So the prophets of Baal cried with a louder voice and cut themselves with swords and knives as was their custom. Their blood flowed all over them. (1 Kings 18:21-28)

Seymour paused and looked up, noticing that Jeremy's attention was beginning to fade. "You see, the prophets of Baal were powerless and not because they didn't try hard enough. It's because their god wasn't powerful enough and flat out wasn't there. Elijah wants to make that clear. Elijah doesn't want the people to think that he's somehow more powerful than these other prophets—as if it's all about him. The battle for the hearts of Israel was not between prophets but between gods. And so Elijah does something surprising. He calls for the Israelites to butcher and prepare the second bull and place it on wood on top of the altar of the Lord and then he digs a trench around the altar."

Looking down, Seymour cleared his throat and continued to read:

> "Fill four jars with water and pour it on the sacrifice and on the wood," he commanded. "Do it a second time!" he said. So they did it a second time. "Do it a third time!" And so they did it a third time. The water flowed around the altar, and even the trench filled with water." (18:33b-35)

Seymour paused again, looked at Jeremy who was still perplexed as to why any of this mattered, and then asked, "Do you realize that Elijah just removed any possibility of his own success? Any hope the people had that Elijah could conjure a spark is removed from the realm of possibility. He wanted to make clear that what was about to happen wasn't about his power but about God's. And that's why he prays this prayer":

> "Lord, the God of Abraham, Isaac, and Israel, let it be known today that you are God in Israel and that I am your servant. I have done all these things at your instructions. Answer me, LORD! Answer me so that this people will know that you, LORD, are the real God and that you can change their hearts." (18:36b-37)

"Who could change their hearts?" Seymour asked almost in a shout, "Who?"

"Um, the Lord," Jeremy responded.

"Yes, the Lord! The Lord is the only one who could change their hearts. Not the teachers and prophets of Israel, not Elijah. Just God. And guess what?" Seymour found his place and began reading again:

> Then the LORD's fire fell; it consumed the sacrifice, the wood, the stones, and the dust. It even licked up the water in the trench!

All the people saw this and fell on their faces. "The LORD is the real God! The LORD is the real God!" they exclaimed." (18:38-39)

Intrigued by Seymour's excitement, Jeremy was nevertheless still perplexed as to what this story had to do with anything, so he just stared at Seymour and waited for him to explain. Seymour got the hint.

"You see, Jeremy, you have about as much chance of igniting the hearts and faith of young people as old Elijah did igniting the sopping wet firewood of that altar. Your programs, whether Sunday school or otherwise, aren't the problem. The difference between you and Elijah is that he knew he was dealing with an impossible situation. Impossible . . . impossible . . . ," Seymour trailed off and stared for a moment at Jeremy. Then he set down his coffee before becoming very quiet.

"Impossible. Unless God acts, unless the Holy Spirit shows up and does something. Your job, Jeremy, is merely to build altars of wet firewood. That's all your Sunday school lessons are supposed to be. It's all they can be. It takes the Spirit of God to ignite them. You need to know far less about trying to convince young people of faith and far more about how to put them into times and places and spaces where we're pretty sure they're likely to encounter the fiery, passionate, transforming God. Let The Teacher teach. Let The Teacher transform. You, however, are not The Teacher. Primarily, you're supposed to be the one who brings students to Jesus—the one who brings students into spaces and places where the Lord can transform their hearts and minds. We do not turn the hearts of youth to God, but we can prepare them to be enlivened by the Spirit of God and for dead religion to become living faith. Transforming faith ultimately depends upon God. You and your efforts are not the hope for transforming youth. Elijah recognized his job was twofold: place the wood upon the altar and pray."

The question for those of us interested in forming the faith of young people is this: How do we go about preparing the altar?

Jeremy thought for a moment, taking in what Seymour was saying and then asked: "So how do I do that? How do I bring students to Jesus, and how do I put students in the times and spaces where God works?"

"Oh, there are many different ideas about that because, of course, God doesn't always work in the same way," explained Seymour. "God doesn't always touch our hearts and transform us in the same times and places. The problem is that most of our teaching assumes that God only works in one particular way. If I say 'teaching,' you're likely to say 'classroom.' Moreover, you're likely to think about having a lesson with a point—a big idea and an application. You're likely to think of opening up students' heads and pouring in knowledge." Seymour looked at Jeremy sternly, then continued: "And, that's certainly one way, and the classroom is one place where the Holy Spirit might work. But there are other ways, times, and places where we might lead students to encounter the Holy Spirit. However, it's to our own detriment if we think teaching and formation of faith must happen strictly in a classroom and strictly in one stale way."

"Like what? What other places and ways?" Jeremy asked. He was intrigued at this point because he hoped that what Seymour was about to tell him was the key to finally killing Sunday school once and for all, since surely Sunday school *wasn't* the place.

"Patience. We'll get there, I think," said Seymour. "When are you coming back to see me?"

"Um, well, I didn't know I was," said Jeremy honestly, even as his hopes for keeping this to a one-time meeting suddenly faded.

"No, no. You need to come back. I'm an old man and we can't do this all in one day," Seymour chided. "What's today?" he asked.

"Monday," said Jeremy.

"Then Wednesday. Come back Wednesday," instructed Seymour. "Oh, and I have something for you," Seymour said as he glanced around the room looking for something. "Somewhere." He went over to a bookcase and began searching the shelves, finally bending to the lowest shelf. "Here!" he exclaimed, pulling a dusty book from the shelf and handing it to Jeremy. It looked like an old library book and was hardbound with a solid blue cloth cover. The only printing on the outside was a single word, the author's name, embossed in gold on the spine: MATHETAI.

"I wrote that book long ago," said Seymour matter of factly. "Read chapter 1 and come back to see me on Wednesday." And with that, Seymour jumped up and walked Jeremy to the door.

Walking down the hallway away from Seymour's room, Jeremy's mind buzzed with what had just transpired. *Did he just give me homework? I hardly did homework in college and I'm not going to start now*, he thought as he settled back into his car, throwing Seymour's blue book into the backseat.

Yet, on the drive home, despite his dismissive thoughts, Jeremy couldn't get Seymour's words out of his head, leading him to think out loud: "I'm not the teacher. The Holy Spirit is The Teacher. I guess that makes me like the coordinator, facilitator, or assistant to what the Holy Spirit wants to do in the lives of teenagers."

There was something both freeing and terrifying about this idea. If his job was to understand the ways that the Holy Spirit was likely to encounter the teenagers in his ministry and put them in proximity to the work of the Spirit, then he wanted to be able to do his job well. He'd certainly never thought of teaching Sunday school, youth group, or anything else with that purpose in mind.

In fact, he'd never thought about anything he did in youth ministry as cooperating with the Holy Spirit or putting youth in touch with the work of God. He'd always suspected that it was his job to form teenagers' faith in God, and he had carried that weight firmly on his shoulders.

But now he wondered, *Maybe it's God who forms faith in teenagers and I get the privilege to watch, be awed by God, and used along the way.* He mulled over that thought. Maybe it was too simple, but one thing was clear: Seymour's ideas made him want to know more. *Fine,* Jeremy thought to himself reluctantly as he pulled into the church parking lot, *I'll read chapter 1.*

CHAPTER 1: THE INSTRUCTIONAL APPROACH

W ith a cup of coffee in one hand and the blue book Seymour had given him in the other, Jeremy settled into the overstuffed chair in his office. He was disappointed to find that the first several pages had withered and fallen out of the book at some point long ago, leaving empty threads of dried yellow binding glue along the inside of the spine. *I can't believe I'm bothering to read this*, Jeremy thought as he eyed the book and took a sip of coffee. *This book feels ancient and I'm trying to teach teenagers today, not decades ago. But, oh well, I'll give it a chance. Maybe.* Just as Seymour had instructed, Jeremy thumbed to chapter 1 and began reading ...

To teach is to create a space in which obedience to truth is practiced. —Parker Palmer, *To Know as We Are Known*

THE WEIGHT OF THE TASK

The instructional approach is the dominant philosophy for studying the Bible and forming the faith of teenagers in most churches. Drawing from educational theory and educational philosophy, those who take an instructional approach tend to emphasize the similarity between learning religion and any other content. In fact, as one Christian educator has argued: "Religion teaching

1

is basically no different from any other kind of teaching. Nor is the learning of religion basically different from any other kind of learning."[1] As such, advocates for taking an instructional approach in forming youth in the faith structure their curriculum and techniques to replicate the educational research and practices that guide public educational practices. The aim or goal of instruction is to bring the student to an understanding of the content being taught. If the goal of understanding is accomplished, then the hopeful outcome for the student will be application of the content to the student's personal life and behavior. Over time the student should mature in faith, evidenced by changes in the student's life choices and actions and resulting in the student becoming progressively more mature in Christian faith and life.

It is the role of the teacher in the instructional approach to assess student needs and capacities and then to choose content and methods for instruction that will enable student growth.

As one educator has described it, "the teacher is to consider what knowledge and understanding the student has gained, how faith and thought have been integrated, what Christian values and attitudes have been acquired, what level of theological maturity is evidenced, and what patterns or operations of living have been formed."[2] With all these things in mind, the teacher then structures the next learning experience for students, which most often occurs in a formal classroom or designated learning environment.

If this sounds heady and potentially over-structured, then advocates of an instructional approach might actually rejoice because many of them lament the way in which the teaching efforts of youth ministry often suffer from lack of planning, intentionality, and spiral growth structures. Most tragic, say advocates of an instructional approach, is the poor preparation we give to those we call teachers. In an instructional framework, the teacher is an incredibly important component, and yet most churches spend more time and money on curriculum than preparing teachers to actually teach the curriculum! While the content that is taught is vitally important to advocates of an instructional approach, what is equally important are trained and quality teachers who understand the weight of the task they have been given and who approach the teaching moment with both prayer and preparation.

As one student of youth ministry observed, "I think the church not only does a very poor job of teaching, but an even worse job of bringing up effective teachers."[3] Those who take an instructional approach to opening the Bible with teenagers advocate for four important keys to the success of the approach:

- Teaching teenagers what the Bible says, or a focus on content;
- Bringing students to understand (and trust) the content of Scripture;
- Helping students recognize how the Bible should apply or make a difference in everyday life;
- Equipping and preparing teachers for their task.

The instructional approach shouldn't be confused with just schooling; one can utilize an instructional approach to opening the Bible with teenagers outside of a classroom. The instructional approach isn't determined by the context in which it occurs, nor even by the teaching methods that are employed, but rather by the goal of the approach and the desired outcome for students.

Anchoring the instructional approach is a belief that the truth of Scripture, if delivered to young people, can instigate a change of mind and heart. Scripture needs to be handled by an experienced interpreter so that it can be made understandable to youth. The teacher, or those writing the curriculum, act as interpreters who pre-chew the Word and break it down so that it can be meaningful to youth and they can then determine how Scripture "applies" to their lives. The teacher is meant to pinpoint in Scripture the truth that needs to be communicated and to then present it in such a way that the student can grasp it, understand it, and thus live in light of God's Word.

When approaching teaching from an instructional approach, the point is to teach the truth of Scripture in a way that can be applied to one's life. Therefore, action steps or some kind of "take-home point" are not uncommon, though application should ideally be more interactive than presenting students with canned responses about how the Scripture's truth applies to the individual and personal life of the student.

THE IMPORTANCE OF THE TEACHER IN THE INSTRUCTIONAL APPROACH

From the vantage of the instructional approach, the teacher is crucially important as the one who brings truth before students. The teacher determines the content to be learned, known, and investigated. Not only will the teacher select the Scripture to be examined but also the teacher selects the particular points of understanding that students will be moved toward, as well as the basic contours of how the Scripture likely applies to the students' lives.

The instructional approach tends to flow from the banking model of education. In the banking model the instructor has knowledge that needs to be deposited into the heads of students. Teaching is a transfer of knowledge and, if that transfer of knowledge is performed, then the student will be able to move toward grasping and understanding that knowledge. The learner is one who needs to receive knowledge of the truth and respond to that truth.

Instruction begins by the teacher providing knowledge and explanation to the student: "This is the reason that ...," or, "Here's what should happen when ...." In an instructional framework, the interpretations, understandings, and the views of the teacher (and community) are passed along to the student, shaping the student's ways of knowing, the student's discrete knowledge, and the student's understanding.

An instructional approach to opening the Bible with youth "focuses on the teacher and on teaching responsibility more than on the student."[4] This is not to say that the student is unimportant, but rather that the success of an instructional approach depends significantly on the skill and preparation of the teacher. If the teacher doesn't know how to teach, if the teacher is unskilled in handling Scripture, or if the teacher doesn't have his or her life and knowledge in order, then the instructional approach falls apart.

Since the role of the teacher is so important in this approach, there is great respect for the training of teachers. If we would never consider sending an untrained teacher into a public school classroom to teach middle school math, then why would we ever consider sending such a person into a church classroom to teach middle schoolers the Christian faith? Consequently, robust training and preparation of teachers is of crucial importance so that they are well-versed in the language, beliefs, rhythms, and reasons of the faith community and in their knowledge of the Bible. It is through the faithful and informed action of a teacher that students will be guided to Scripture, come to understand Scripture, and be led to consider how they might apply its truth to their lives in obedience.

THE INSTRUCTIONAL APPROACH AIMS AT UNDERSTANDING

While to instruct means "to furnish with knowledge or information" (*Oxford English Dictionary*), instruction should not be conceived as brainwashing or "unreflective 'passing on' of static propositions to be received as correct doctrine."[5] Instead, instruction is about "giving reasons, evidence, arguments, and so forth, for the purpose of helping another understand or arrive at the truth."[6] The key word here is *understanding*. The aim or goal of instruction is not rote memorization, or the ability to regurgitate, but for the student to understand. In turn, that understanding will enable the student to apply the Scripture to her or his life.

Understanding does not come from an accumulation of facts. We do not say that someone understands merely because the person knows. For example, in school I memorized pi to 40 digits on a challenge from my seventh grade math teacher. I could recite it flawlessly, but knowing pi didn't affect the reality that I had no idea what pi was used for and no idea how to employ it. In the end I had the knowledge of pi, but without understanding it was just random digits. Therefore, understanding moves us beyond mere knowledge of facts to perceiving the meaning of the facts.

For example, we don't normally use the phrase "it dawned on her" to speak about someone learning facts for the first time. In fact, it could be that she's known these facts for years and years. So, to say "it dawned on her" is to say that the facts she already knows suddenly come together with new force and meaning. She grasps the meaning of these facts for herself, for her world, and for the other things she knows. That's understanding.

> **When we talk about "the light bulb going on" for students, what we're often trying to express is the idea of students moving from merely a point of knowledge to a point of personal understanding. This is the basic goal of the instructional approach.**

Along these lines, one particular power of the instructional approach is in leading youth to a clarity of belief. We need to help students clarify what they believe, which is not the same as telling them what to believe. If done well, the instructional approach doesn't lead to passive students but to young people who are actively *thinking* about and questioning their faith, interrogating Scripture, and clarifying what it means and what it doesn't. Teaching from an instructional approach will introduce students to content, along with helping them think through and understand what they believe and why.

What is the primary way we might bring students to understanding? Sharing knowledge and content with students is important, but those who take an instructional approach also believe it is crucial that students are made to think about this knowledge as the gateway to understanding. If operating in an instructional frame, we should gear each lesson, each educational encounter, to draw students into mental activity. Instruction that passively engages students in only listening and regurgitating isn't actually instruction at all; rather, the task of the teacher in an instructional framework is to hand over content to the student in such a way that the student is pressed and prodded to turn it over in the mind—cogitate about it, debate about it, think about it—and ultimately come to true understanding. This might involve getting students to truly think by weighing, assessing, or discussing the content at hand. It's in such discussions that students encounter Aha! moments, understanding arises, and the instructional approach bears fruit. It's not enough to have students come away having heard your big idea for the lesson at hand. It's not even enough if they can come back next week and still remember the big idea for last week's lesson. Rather, taking an instructional approach to teaching means focusing on moving youth toward understanding—and the only clear way to get them there is to get them thinking!

AN INSTRUCTIONAL APPROACH LEADS TO APPLICATION

While the aim of teaching the Bible using an instructional approach is to lead youth toward understanding, the desired outcome is to see them regulate their lives in knowledge of the truth.[7] Their knowledge and understanding of the truth is just the foundation that leads them toward determining how they might apply that truth and live it out. Application is crucial. A student gaining understanding alone is not enough; if the application of Scripture is not emphasized, then the wheels fall off the instructional approach.

1

Application ultimately involves making a determination of how one might be obedient to the truth of Scripture given the unique circumstances of one's personal and cultural context. An instructional approach should create an environment in which obedience to truth is encouraged. Application is a matter of helping students see how they might align their lives with truth in the way that the needle of a compass aligns itself to magnetic north. We hope to see them apply the truth of Scripture by bringing their lives into compliance with what is true, beautiful, and good. To do this, we first bring students to consider the truth of Scripture, then we bring them to an understanding of the meaning of the truth, and then we lead them to consider how truth is to be applied obediently in their individual and contextual life experiences.

Obedience to the truth doesn't come about by merely memorizing the truth; obedience to the truth can only arise where there is also an understanding of the truth.

How should application be generated in an instructional approach lesson? While it is possible to hand students an application point, and this often happens in instructional approach curriculum, it is far better to help students wrestle with the scriptural passage under examination in order to help them arrive at an understanding and application of the Scripture that they own and embrace. The teacher should always provide the basic contours for application and point and prod in the right direction, in keeping with the instructional approach belief that the teacher is the primary source of knowledge for the student. Yet, if instruction is truly to lead toward application, then students must be active in the process of determining application.

It can't be overstated how important the application aspect of the lesson should be when teaching in the instructional approach. Yet, almost invariably the application portion of the lesson is tacked on to the end and rushed in the last few minutes of the learning session when student attention has already started to flee the room. This is a grave mistake because it relegates the desired outcome of the entire lesson to an afterthought.

If we hope to see students become obedient to the words and commands of God revealed in Scripture, then why would we give the portion of the lesson that is directly involved in this desired outcome such little time and prominence in our lessons? Following are at least two common reasons why the all-important application is nearly sidelined or tacked on as an afterthought.

- **We tend to be more comfortable dealing with the facts of biblical content than we are with the potentially messy aspects of discussing application in the lives of students.**

This makes teachers feel insecure and so a common defense is to avoid giving much time to application. If this is your tendency as a teacher, I would suggest stepping outside of your comfort zone, because your lessons might seem well received, but they are unlikely to truly impact students until pondering the application of Scripture is given appropriate time and space in your teaching.

- **We tend to tack application to the end of a lesson because sharing predigested application points requires little time.**

Telling students how to apply the Scripture in three easy steps takes only a few minutes. However, it also turns out that such an approach is not very effective for helping students embrace and apply the truth of Scripture. If your pattern as a teacher is to give quick application points, I would challenge you to expand the application portion of an instructional lesson into a true dialogue with time for creative thought. While it might make you feel good handing students a nicely crafted application point, the potential for meaningful obedience to the Scripture comes from students thinking about and tossing around potential ways the Scripture applies to their lives and world.

Ensuring that students wrestle with both understanding the content of Scripture while also applying it to their lives is at the heart of a well-crafted instructional approach lesson. Both aspects are needed, and it is imperative to give neither short shrift. A good instructional approach lesson will engage students in discussing and understanding the facts of Scripture, but it also will give ample time for discussing application. Using poignant questions and prompts to help students think through the Scripture and its possible applications to their lives is as crucial as finding ways to help students think about the Scripture in the first place.

ENCOUNTERING DIVINE ACTION THROUGH OBEDIENCE TO SCRIPTURE

Behind every approach to opening the Bible with teenagers is a particular belief, or set of beliefs, about the nature and work of the Holy Spirit. Christians believe that the Holy Spirit is the originator, teacher, and transformer of faith. Faith does not come about by human effort. It is not possible for human teachers, no matter how trained or skilled, to instigate faith. As teachers, we might be able to nurture faith, encourage it, or at least point others in the direction of faith, but it is the fire and power of God's Spirit at work that brings faith.

However, don't be fooled into thinking that humans have no role in faith development. We certainly do make a difference, and the human role might best be conceived as cooperating with divine activity by bringing students into spaces and places in which the Holy Spirit often transforms hearts and minds. We, of course, cannot control when and how the Holy Spirit works. There are no limits and nothing is impossible with God. However, it is possible to point to some usual ways and places that Christians believe the Holy Spirit works.

When we teach in the context of Christian ministry, we are always seeking to bring human activity into association and cooperation with God's activity. It is not our teaching that ultimately effects change in students; rather our efforts should be aligned to work with the ways of the Spirit as Teacher and Transformer. Therefore, in order to say anything about human action, we must first discern and articulate our understanding of God's action:

- How do we believe the Holy Spirit is at work in the world?
- How does the Holy Spirit teach and transform individuals?

Only when we have considered divine action can we speak faithfully about how we might respond and cooperate as human actors. Thus, each of the various teaching approaches surveyed in this book relates to a different conception about the way God works; the nature of what "teaching" entails for each approach is determined by these different ways of conceiving God's action.

It's important to note the following:

Change your theory of divine action, and logically, your teaching approach must change as well.

The problem is that while it's common to hold various theories of divine action simultaneously, most youth workers tend to teach from a single approach. If we truly believe the Holy Spirit works in diverse ways, then it's time to diversify our teaching approaches in hopes of better cooperating with the Spirit. One of the goals of this book is to help you consider your personal beliefs about ways in which students are likely to encounter the work of God as Teacher and to, therefore, expand the teaching approaches from which you work.

1

With all this in mind, the theory of divine action operative for many who advocate an instructional approach is one that sees God's action located in the truth of the words of Scripture. According to this perspective, embedded in Scripture by the work of the Holy Spirit, is truth for living. When humans bring their lives and behavior into compliance with the truth of Scripture, they are encountering the transforming work of God.[8] The Spirit has primarily spoken and worked in producing and preserving the Scriptures as a source for life, a measuring stick against which we should compare our lives. While the Holy Spirit is still at work awakening and wooing faith in the hearts of individuals, if we want to bring our students into an encounter with the work of God, then bringing them to consider the truth of Scripture and its application for their lives is crucially important. If the understanding of divine action just discussed resonates with your experience and theology, then it is likely you'll have an affinity for the instructional approach.

What value is there in recognizing the theory of divine action that undergirds an approach to opening the Bible with teenagers? Primarily the value is in recognizing the ways human action can go off the rails by forgetting that our action is meant to cooperate with God's action.

For example, if the power in instruction is bringing students into contact with truth for living inspired by the Holy Spirit, then our actions fall short when we fail to bring students to a clear understanding of the ways in which Scripture applies to their lives. The role of human teachers in this case is to help uncover and make understandable the truth for living found in the Bible. If the Bible is neglected in our teaching, or if we open the Bible and teach students the content while failing to bring them to understanding and application of the truth, then we have not fully cooperated with the activity of God.

1

TAKING THE INSTRUCTIONAL APPROACH OUTSIDE THE BOX

Even though the instructional approach dominates the practice of teaching in youth ministry, we don't always do it well, and so making some important shifts in the way we undertake instruction can move teaching outside the norm.

First, in an effort to make instructional forms of teaching easily accessible to untrained teachers and leaders, the vast majority of curriculum publishers strip the approach of its power and ultimately its meaning (and effectiveness) by crafting lessons that move students toward knowledge without understanding or thinking and toward trite application points tacked onto the end of the lesson. If you wish to employ the instructional approach, be sure that the curriculum you're using entices students to actually think and wrestle with the major points for understanding identified in the lesson's objective. If it doesn't, then modify the curriculum by employing a teaching method and strategy that will move students toward understanding through thinking.

Second, reject the tendency of instructional curriculum to provide students with trite application. Instead, ensure that your lesson invites students into robust discussion of the Scripture passage and reflection of the application of the truth to their lives. Often, with time ticking down in the class, we unveil an application and go around the circle to ask students how they might apply this Scripture in their individual lives. If you've gotten the deer in the headlights stare at this point, then you're not alone. Rather than revealing an application point at the end of the teaching session, a good instructional approach lesson weaves application throughout, so that students come to understand the Scripture, believe that it needs to be applied to their lives, and discuss and think about the application progressively throughout the lesson.

1

If you're presenting youth with an application, you also are preventing youth from being invested in the application, and it will be so thinly held that it's likely they won't remember it by the time they get home.

In contrast, if your teaching time wraps understanding and application together, working on one and then the other in a cyclical fashion, while inviting students to be in creative thought and dialogue about both, then you're more likely to send students out both understanding the Scripture and owning the application.

Another problem teachers encounter when trying to employ the instructional approach is failing to focus on the specific aspects of the passage about which students should come to an understanding. A good instructional lesson doesn't just expose students to every jot and tittle in the scriptural text; rather, there's something specific in the text that teenagers need to understand so they can apply it to their lives. In the instructional approach, it is the role of the teacher to find a clear focus on what she or he hopes students will understand about the scriptural passage being considered. It's then the role of the teacher to employ various methods of exploration and examination to move teenagers toward understanding as they think about the Scripture. Teachers who operate well in the instructional approach make sure that everything they add to their lesson is building toward the core concepts they've identified as crucial.

Closely related, teachers should ensure that the lesson focuses firmly on the aspects of the Scripture pertinent to the application. It's possible to spend incredible amounts of time trying to bring students to understand aspects of Scripture that in the end have no bearing on the application of the truth of that Scripture to their lives. Similarly, if you're taking time to play some kind of learning game, doing a roleplay, or having students retell the story— whatever the method—ensure that it is leading them toward greater understanding of the aspects of the text that are necessary for application.

. . . .

Finishing the last of his coffee with a gulp, Jeremy dropped the blue book onto the side table with a thud. "Made it," he said aloud to himself. Though some of what he'd read resonated with him, there was much he didn't quite understand. The instructional approach certainly described the way he tended to think about the teaching task, but he'd never thought about it in the kind of detail Seymour had described. He was intrigued by the discussion on the work of the Holy Spirit and trying to cooperate with the Spirit, but he also was confused by this and didn't truly understand why it mattered.

As Jeremy thought about his own teaching in light of what he just read, he clearly could see places where Seymour would criticize his efforts. Maybe, in fact, part of the lackluster response he received from students was due to the fact that he fell into some of the traps that Seymour identified. He was certainly guilty in his teaching of spending considerable time focusing on parts of the scriptural passage that had nothing to do with what he wanted students to actually learn; often he did this simply to ensure that his lessons filled the full hour. Yet, even at the same time he was trying to stretch his lessons to an hour, he realized he more often than not tacked a quick application point onto the end of his teaching time, sending students out the door with a trivial "take-home point."

Looking over at his desk where he'd stacked curriculum for the next several weeks of class, Jeremy decided to see what would happen if he looked at next week's lesson through Seymour's eyes. What would he change about the curriculum if anything? He grabbed the printed teacher guide for the prodigal son lesson and began reading and marking places where he saw problems.

Most strikingly Jeremy realized how the lesson was crafted to prevent students from thinking. The teaching strategies suggested would keep students active—a skit to perform and a game to play—but none actually prompted students to think about the content he was supposed to share with them. Rather, it was just a matter of presenting the information in unique ways. Also, sure enough, there was an application tacked onto the end of the lesson. Students were asked to copy down the application, but without discussion or exploration.

Sighing a little, Jeremy decided he'd take a whack at modifying the parts of the lesson he figured Seymour would find lacking. He grabbed a pen and some paper and went to work. He wasn't exactly sure what he was doing, but it was worth the effort to become a better teacher.

The lesson, as it was written, opened with a funny game in which students would push against one another's hands; the point of the game was metaphorical—an attempt to illustrate that we tend to resist (or push back) on God's grace. The main point of the lesson was focused on the younger brother and the way he resisted his father's grace and love, which was nevertheless extended to him even after he had run away and squandered his inheritance. Yet, as Jeremy looked over the lesson and researched a few Bible commentaries on the passage, he began to see another theme: the rejection of the father's grace by the older son. The older son was called to be an agent and participant in the father's grace ("slaughter the fattened calf"), but he resisted being party to extending grace. "Wow, we really need to think together about the way that we're resistant in cooperating with the grace that God extends to others! God is giving them grace, and we're often giving people grief," Jeremy thought aloud. He realized quickly this truth needed to be the focal point he wanted to drive home for the students, but he also realized doing this called for a more significant revision to the curriculum than he'd originally planned.

With this new teaching idea in mind, Jeremy continued to look through the guide for activities and teaching points he could keep. There was a skit activity in which students would reenact the prodigal son story. It felt like a colossal waste of time to have students act out the whole story for no apparent reason. *But wait,* Jeremy thought, as the words of Seymour's blue book popped to mind: "Make sure the activities are focused on the point of Scripture you're trying to draw out." He realized he could salvage the skit, make it meaningful even, by asking half the students to write a skit that demonstrated an answer to this question: *What would the older brother have done in action and attitude if he had decided to participate in the father's grace?* Additionally, he decided to add another skit performed by the other students that was to answer this question: *What are the thoughts of the older brother as he protests and rejects the father's grace?*

Some other aspects of the lesson were OK. There was a group artistic response and a closing prayer they would recite together. But other components were clearly missing, such as a way to move youth from knowledge of the passage toward understanding. He didn't want to stand and lecture, so he came up with some questions he believed would draw the students toward a deeper understanding of the father's grace and the older son's resistance to grace, the key aspect of his focal Scripture. Additionally, these questions would hearken back to some of the insight students should have gained during the skits:

- What does the father's grace look like in this passage? How is it portrayed?
- What can we believe about God's grace as a result of this parable?
- What would participating in the father's grace have looked like for the older son in both actions and attitude?
- Why do you think it was difficult for the older son to participate as an agent in the father's grace for the younger son?

- What makes it difficult for you to be an agent and proclaimer of God's grace to others? Are you ever held back by feelings similar to those experienced by that older brother?

Jeremy then developed an application activity for the end of the lesson that asked students to think of one person for whom they might be an agent or proclaimer of God's grace. This was an important question, but the words of the blue book popped into his mind again, "Weave the application throughout." Jeremy realized he'd resorted to old habits by tacking the application onto the end of the lesson. So, he went back through the lesson and modified his teaching plan by giving every student an index card at the beginning of the lesson and asking them to write the name of one person they know who is in need of God's grace. He decided he'd spend a little time orienting them to God's grace so they could answer this question. Then, he also modified his closing question: *Thinking back to the person whose name you listed at the beginning of the session, what are some concrete ways you can be an agent or proclaimer of God's grace in that person's life?* Jeremy planned to find additional ways to draw students' attention to extending grace to these people at various points in the lesson, and he'd close with a prayer asking God to empower them with the ability to overcome their stumbling blocks to grace.

"Wow, I think this is much better," he said to himself as he leaned back in his chair after a lengthy period of revision. "I'll send it to Seymour and see what he says."

· · · ·

"Very good. Interesting. Hmm," Seymour mumbled to himself as he looked over Jeremy's revised lesson plan. Jeremy had dropped by Oak Harbor Assisted Living to say hello to Seymour—but mostly to find out what the old man thought of his Sunday school lesson on the prodigal son.

After a bit, Seymour said: "I'm impressed at how your application is woven throughout the lesson and how it helps students think for themselves about how the passage applies. Additionally, I'd say you've done well at using a variety of teaching methods to move students toward understanding an aspect of the passage. Also, I think your strategy for the skits just might work."

"What do you mean by strategy and teaching method? I was trying to stay within the instructional approach you described in your book. Did I not do that?" asked Jeremy.

"Oh, you did that very well. Maybe I just need to do a better job of explaining my terms," Seymour said apologetically. "Approaches, methods, and strategies are all different, and it's important to have a clear understanding of each. An approach is defined by a particular aim or goal. So, because you crafted this lesson with an instructional approach in mind, the goal is for students to understand an important aspect of the passage and apply it to their lives. If you had begun with a different approach, then your goals would be different. Some approaches aim for students to discern the voice of God, other approaches aim to awaken teenagers to oppression and spur them to action, and still other approaches aim at helping students to interpret their lives in light of the scriptural story. The point is:

The approach you start with always defines your aim and should guide the methods you employ.

"Now, a method is a way of actually teaching that's used to accomplish the goal—such as discussion, lecture, debate, and roleplay—they are all methods," Seymour explained. "There are literally hundreds of different methods that can be used in teaching, but the way they're used will always be determined by the goals or aims of your teaching approach. In this lesson you use skit as a teaching method specifically to help students focus on one aspect of the story. Why? Because the goal of a lesson crafted in the instructional approach is not for students to perfectly remember each part of the story but rather to help them understand a particular aspect of the passage and apply it. However, if your goal was different—say, having students interpret the meaning of their lives through an encounter with the story—then the way you use the skit method would likely be different. In that case you probably would have wanted students to perform the whole story in skit form.

"Finally, strategy is a very specific way of employing a particular teaching method. So in this lesson you employ the method of skit to help students focus on one part of the story, and the specific strategy you employ is having students imagine what could have happened if the older brother had acted differently. The important thing is that it's clear to me why you do this: You use the skit to help students get into the head of the older brother who was resistant to cooperating with the father's grace. And that's important because you want students to understand their own resistance to cooperating with God's grace to others and to ultimately apply this new understanding to their lives by making a change in how they respond to others.

"Likewise, you use the method of discussion with the particular strategy of helping students understand the nature of grace and the reasons someone might be resistant to proclaiming and announcing God's grace. Your discussion strategy moves students to first understand and then toward applying the Scripture to their lives.

"The fact is that pretty much any approach out there can employ discussion and skit as teaching methods. The important thing is that you tailored your method and strategies to be in service to the goals of the instructional approach you're trying to embody in this lesson."

Jeremy felt some pride at Seymour's words. He'd successfully revised this lesson, and he felt much better about what he would be teaching. He'd also earned Seymour's approval, and he'd done what Pastor Jack had asked him to do—scoring points with the home team in the process. He was thankful that his time with Seymour hadn't been wasted; he'd learned a lot.

"So I'll be seeing you next week, I'm sure," Seymour said to Jeremy as he rose from his chair.

"What? Next week?" Jeremy asked, feeling confused.

"We have four more approaches to study, so I say it's best we get going," Seymour said with a twinkle in his eye. He grabbed the blue book that Jeremy had returned and dog-eared a page a few chapters in. Seymour handed the book back to Jeremy on his way out the door, saying with a chuckle: "You're not going to get rid of me that easily. Here's an assignment from your teacher. Read it."

Download the full leader's guide for Jeremy's instructional approach lesson on the prodigal son, including all liturgical elements, by visiting *http://www.youthministrypartners.com/tob*.

Endnotes

[1] From James Michael Lee in *Contemporary Approaches to Christian Education*, by Jack L. Seymour and Donald E. Miller (Abingdon Press, 1982); pages 16-17.

[2] From *Contemporary Approaches*; page 18.

[3] From *Teaching That Makes a Difference: How to Teach for Holistic Impact*, by Dan Lambert (Zondervan/Youth Specialties, 2004); page 15.

[4] From *Contemporary Approaches*; page 38.

[5] From *Contemporary Approaches*; pages 38, 39.

[6] From *Contemporary Approaches*; page 39.

[7] Discussed in *Contemporary Approaches*; page 45.

[8] For more on this view of divine action, see "Postscript: Reflecting on Method—Youth Ministry as Practical Theology," in *The Theological Turn in Youth Ministry*, by Andrew Root and Kenda Creasy Dean (InterVarsity Press, 2011); pages 218-236.

CHAPTER 2: THE COMMUNITY OF FAITH APPROACH

The sound of the coffee shop melted away as Jeremy put his headphones on and sat back to read his latest homework assignment from Seymour. He was not happy about being assigned to read something for a second week in a row, and he was pleased when he noticed this chapter was a bit shorter than the first. With coffee in hand—for he was certain he wouldn't be staying awake without it—he launched in ...

> To teach is to create a space in which the community of truth is practiced. —Parker Palmer, *Exploring the Inner Landscape of a Teacher's Life*

THE GOSPEL IN MOTION

The community of faith approach contrasts sharply with almost all aspects of the instructional approach introduced in the previous chapter. This approach eschews the classroom and views it largely as a contrived environment for learning. Instead, it views the actions of the community as both the content and the context for learning.

The community of faith approach begins with the assumption that when we worship, baptize, and partake in the Lord's Supper, we're teaching and forming Christians. If there are young Christians

2

along as we greet one another, love one another, or serve in our community, then we are forming them. When the pastor preaches, when we pray together, or when we read and discuss Scripture together—in those times we are forming youth and teaching them the faith because they're learning what the gospel looks like in motion.

The community of faith approach discards what Stuart Cummings-Bond once called "The One-Eared Mickey Mouse" model of youth ministry.[1] This common mode of ministry views the church as Mickey's head, with youth ministry stuck on the side like Mickey's ear, not having much interaction with the church at all. One way this approach attempts to rectify the Mickey problem is by recognizing that the context of education matters when teaching the faith.

While the instructional approach places considerable emphasis on the teacher's ability to teach content that youth can understand and apply, the community of faith approach recognizes that the context in which learning happens is as important as the content that is learned.

The community of faith approach emphasizes that learning is situated and that the gospel is communicated through lives lived, not merely through words communicated.

Advocates of a community of faith approach are prone to jettison student and teacher language, preferring instead to see youth as apprentices of the community. In recent years the phrase *student ministry* has gained traction among churches, but one of the consequences of this type of language is that it tends to treat youth as mere students whose only task and role in the church is to learn until they become adults. Increasingly, however, teenagers don't stick around long enough for this to happen.

On the other hand, the community of faith approach and the apprentice model that fits within it see youth as members of the body of Christ who are learning as they are leading and participating in the midst of the congregation. They do not need to be separated; instead they need to watch their parents, peers, and elders worshiping together, learning together, and living the Christian faith together. So the intended outcome for youth is that they become apprentices, and the goal of the approach is that they are formed in faith by being enculturated, or folded into, the ways and rhythms of the community.

SITUATED LEARNING THEORY

It's interesting to consider the community of faith approach in light of the Situated Learning Theory advanced by Jean Lave and Etienne Wagner. Situated learning is a secular theory of education that proceeds on some of the same assumptions as the community of faith approach. Situated Learning Theory assumes we learn as apprentices in a community where we are allowed to have *legitimate peripheral participation*. Each of those words is important to understanding how apprentices are formed, as opposed to the mere formation of students.

> **1. Apprentices are formed when we engage teens in legitimate activity.** An electrician's apprentice doesn't learn by pretending to fix a home's wiring; instead he goes out on the site with a master electrician who teaches him while he assists in the very real act of repairing the wiring. The learning environment is not contrived or created for the apprentice; it's legitimate because it would exist whether the apprentice was present or not. If you think about much of what we do in youth ministry, it exists only because youth exist. Classroom teaching, youth events, and activities are planned—not because that's what the church does naturally—but solely because of youth. In fact,

2

youth are rarely involved in the legitimate activities of the church. We often don't give them a role in the worship and actual life of the church. A community of faith approach to communicating the gospel will recognize the importance of involving youth in legitimate (rather than fabricated) activity.

2. Apprentices are formed when their involvement is peripheral as opposed to the center (and focus) of the activity at hand. Back to our example: The master electrician doesn't thrust the apprentice into the central role of planning the wiring for the whole home. Instead, the apprentice is given peripheral roles with graduated complexity that assist the master electrician along the way. A community of faith approach will recognize that it's important to allow youth to assist in real and important ways in the life of the community without shoving them into premature centrality.

3. Apprentices are formed when they actually participate on an ongoing basis. This is in contrast to the student approach in which "students" merely watch others or learn about what others do. Apprenticeship is active, involving youth in the community's actual practice and life.

Now, let's analyze the common place tradition of Youth Sunday, in light of these concepts from Situated Learning Theory. Your church may have this tradition in which youth are given complete control of the worship service annually or quarterly. How does this practice stack up against *legitimate peripheral participation*?

1. Rather than giving youth ways to participate in worship on an ongoing basis, for nine-tenths of the year they merely watch what's happening during worship. Even though youth are incredibly active on Youth Sunday once a year, this fails the participatory test.

2

2. Instead of youth assisting in *aspects* of worship, we completely hand over the service to them. They are the central focus and they sink or swim alone. So, Youth Sunday fails the peripheral test also.

3. Is the activity legitimate? In one way—yes. Because the community gathers every Sunday for worship, youth are involved in leading an activity in which the community routinely engages. However, Youth Sunday only exists because of youth—so the legitimacy of the worship service as something the community would do anyway is almost overthrown by creating the "youth only" form and structure.

Therefore, Youth Sunday actually fails all three of the tests of apprenticeship as understood by Situated Learning Theory.

SANCTUARY-BASED YOUTH MINISTRY

The community of faith approach borrows much from the wisdom of the apprenticeship model. So, it's going to have a different approach from merely pushing youth into extreme forms of leadership once or twice a year. A community of faith approach could almost be described as *sanctuary-based youth ministry*. This doesn't mean that the sanctuary is the only context for youth ministry. In fact, youth ministry happens as the church lives its life in the world and while youth observe and participate in the adult rhythms and practices of faith. A sanctuary-based youth ministry model recognizes that youth are being formed as apprentices wherever they are, learning the faith by watching and doing. A sanctuary-based model ensures youth are welcomed and invited to participate in the worship of the community.

Sanctuary-based faith formation of youth might include planning aspects of the service to provide explicit instruction on the purposes of the liturgy, thereby fulfilling the biblical mandate that the elements of Christian worship be edifying. Edification is the litmus test for what's in and what's out in Christian worship. For example, the reason the apostle Paul gives for putting limits on speaking in tongues isn't because the practice is weird but because it is not edifying if there is no one to interpret. So, in an increasingly post-Christian world, it makes sense to explain well what we do in our services of worship together and consider how all our practices might be edifying.

THE HOLY SPIRIT AND THE COMMUNITY OF FAITH

The question of how we believe the Holy Spirit is at work and how we can best cooperate with divine activity is important when considering any approach to teaching the Bible or forming the faith of teenagers. The belief that the Holy Spirit is at work in and through the historic and communal practices of the Christian faith is one theory of divine activity that undergirds a community of faith approach. The notion is that God's grace is mediated to us through Christian practices such as Communion, baptism, prayer, service, hospitality, and testimony. In other words, we experience God's grace which brings our faith to life amidst the everyday practices of the Christian faith. Each of these means of grace point to God, but they also bear God's truth and grace within them. So, in this view, the Lord's Supper is not just something we do quarterly while remembering the death of Jesus, but rather the Holy Spirit mediates grace to us through our participation in the meal. Likewise, practices of prayer, fasting, community, and clothing the naked aren't just pious practices that earn us favor with God; they are the very means by which God's transforming grace shapes us, forms us, and flows through us to the world.

Such a view of the Holy Spirit's work naturally leads beyond a strictly instructional approach. While classroom learning can certainly be a context for the Holy Spirit's work, it is not the only, nor primary, practice through which we might encounter God's grace that enlivens and grows our faith. Thus, participation in a variety of practices—specifically historic communal practices of faith—becomes important. As we learn the rhythms of Christian faith in these practices, we also encounter the work of the Holy Spirit. Exposing teenagers to a diversity of practices amidst the body of Christ is our best way of cooperating with the Holy Spirit, according to this approach.

TEACHING IN AND BEYOND THE SANCTUARY

Now, as I mentioned, a community of faith approach goes well beyond the sanctuary. It sees the entirety of the life of the congregation as formational. Aunt Mildred, who sits on the second row (you know her, every church has an older person like her), is doing youth ministry by the way she interacts with youth—or, by the way she ignores them. She's also doing youth ministry in the attitude she takes toward others in the church and the way she relates to them. Youth are constantly watching and being formed by the attitudes and actions of adults in the church. These ways of life are formational, whether they know it or not.

Generally, parents and churches get the kind of faith they model, not the kind of faith they teach about in Sunday school. Practical theologian and youth ministry professor Kenda Creasy Dean highlights the National Study of Youth and Religion's finding that "benign whateverism" describes many teenagers' view of religion: Benign in that it's just kind of there; whateverism in that it doesn't have all that much importance to teens' lives.[2] Additionally, the study noted that the faith of teenagers in America can't really be called Christian as much as it can be called Moralistic Therapeutic Deism (MTD). It's a faith that is about being nice, feeling good, and expecting God to show up only when you need a god. How did we get here? How did teenagers end up with this kind of faith? By watching us, Dean says. It's not that teenagers aren't learning the

2

faith from churches and parents; it's that they're learning too well what we're modeling for them.

As a result, the community of faith approach posits that teaching isn't about finding the right words so that teenagers can understand the faith and apply it. Teaching is a matter of modeling for youth what faith is, what it means, and what it looks like in everyday life. This isn't accomplished by a Sunday school teacher or youth pastor alone. Our lives together as Christians in community translate the gospel into life.

Missiologist Lesslie Newbigin spent most of his life as a Christian missionary in India trying to understand what it meant to proclaim the Christian gospel amongst a people whose frame of reference was so different from a Western, Christian mind-set. Newbigin recognized that words could not make the gospel understandable until there was a community that made the gospel meaningful. He concluded that the Christian community is the hermeneutic of the gospel or the interpretive principle, the Rosetta Stone of Christianity; our lives together as the church make the gospel message and the entirety of the biblical narrative understandable. For Newbigin, the Christian message cannot be easily communicated with propositions; rather it must be embodied in the community that lives, reads, and breathes the Word together.

In terms of learning, the community of faith approach assumes that learners learn by watching, participating, and being immersed in a habitat of faith.

Teaching in the community of faith approach might look like the Orthodox congregation inviting a teenager to swing the censer as they process around the outside of the church building on Easter eve. It might look like the Presbyterian congregation inviting a teenager to lead the prayer of confession. Teaching can happen by including teenagers in the prayers the church prays, the actions the church takes, the love the church shows, and so forth. It does not mean disbanding age-specific youth programs, but it does mean that age-specific programs don't take youth away from real and meaningful interactions with the rest of the congregation where the modeling of Scripture happens through the life of the community.

REVERSING THE FLOW OF YOUTH MINISTRY

How might formal youth ministry efforts (such as youth group) be reconceived using a community of faith approach? The dominant model for youth ministry is to find some willing and interested adults in the congregation who will remove themselves from their adult interactions and make the journey up the stairs, down the stairs, or across the parking lot into the youth area. Our age-specific programs not only separate youth but require a few brave adults also to separate themselves from the larger congregation.

What if we reversed that equation? What if some of our age-specific programming included recruiting a few adults who are involved in various ministries of the congregation and then infusing youth into those ministries. So, we contact Aunt Mildred (remember her?) who happens to work the Thursday soup kitchen for the church, we train her to receive youth into her ministry, and then we send a few youth to help her. She trains them, they work with her, and maybe they even end up doing a Bible study together with the soup kitchen workers. If done right, such a model could breathe life into the congregation and its life together, instead of enlisting the most vibrant people we can find in the church and sucking them out to youth ministry across the parking lot.

THE APPROACH IN PRACTICE

At this point, you're likely wondering what community of faith approach curriculum might look like. The answer is considerably different from an instructional lesson. Take a look at the following ideas:

2

- A family or all-church service project in which youth play a prominent part, and the church interacts around a Scripture that frames their time together;
- A group of teenagers who assist the pastor in developing the sermon, studying and discussing the passage with the pastor, learning and giving back at the same time;
- A discussion guide based on Sunday sermons for parents to use with their teens;
- An all-church retreat that incorporates teens in the planning and execution of the retreat and engages the church in times of learning, worship, preaching, fellowship, and so forth;
- Liturgy that routinely involves students in planning, learning, and leading aspects (but not the entirety) of worship.

Notice that none of these ideas utilize an age-based classroom, and each involves legitimate, peripheral participation. Further, any direct instruction in Scripture is embedded in some other edifice, idea, or program. Rather than creating a contrived environment for teaching Scripture, the Bible—as the document that grounds Christian life—is discussed and lived out in the everyday practices of the church where it has always guided faith.

Let's consider the way the topic of baptism might be explored using the community of faith approach compared to the instructional approach. In an instructional framework, a teacher might sit with a class of teenagers and read a scriptural passage on baptism— let's say Matthew 3, John's baptism of Jesus. They might discuss the meaning of baptism as described in the passage and consider Jesus' reason for seeking baptism or John's reason for baptizing people in the first place. They might pair this with a look at the Great Commission and Jesus' command to go forth and baptize, ultimately concluding with some sort of application that might result in a call for members of the class to be baptized or a call to encourage and support the baptism of others.

2

In contrast, in a community of faith framework, baptism would be a theme explored as teenagers are present at a legitimate practice of the congregation such as an intergenerational worship service. In a Methodist congregation, there might be an infant baptism slated for an upcoming Sunday morning, and a decision is made to focus the congregation on the meaning of baptism that morning. The pastor might prepare a sermon on John's baptism of Jesus. One of the morning Scripture readings might be from Matthew 28, the Great Commission. Those responsible for planning the service might consider various ways to lead congregants in reflecting on their individual baptisms during the liturgy. Children and teenagers might be invited forward during the baptism to witness up close the baptism of this infant and to "remember their own baptism" as the pastor sprinkles not only the baby but also allows water to splash across young people nearby. There might be a testimony given (a decidedly Methodist tradition) by someone who reflects on the meaning of his or her baptism. In such ways an immersive sensory experience of celebrating a baptism amidst the community of faith can be turned into a faith-forming and educating event for teenagers and all in attendance.

In light of this, it should be noted that a community of faith approach works best if it is pursued by the entire church and not just the youth minister in the youth room.

In this approach youth ministry happens in the worship service, in the hallways of the church, at home as parents discuss and model faith, amidst whole-church service projects, and/or during intergenerational Bible studies.

Advocates of a community of faith approach will remind their congregations that every member is doing youth ministry all the time, because whenever and wherever young people are present, ministry to youth is happening. Since youth are always watching and learning, every member of the congregation becomes a teacher and modeler of faith, for better or worse.

2

A QUESTION ABOUT INSTRUCTION

A common question about the community of faith approach is whether instruction can be used at all. And the answer is absolutely. What defines any teaching approach is the aim of the approach, not the specific methods utilized to teach. Therefore, instruction can be used as a method of teaching as long as it supports the goal and outcome of the community of faith approach.

In fact, if a congregation believes that socialization into the practices of the community is enough, without some form of overt instruction toward understanding of the ways of the community, then teenagers can end up learning merely dead religion. I've seen plenty of congregations where children and youth are included in the liturgy and ways of life of the congregation without fully grasping what they're doing or why. I recall times when I've watched young acolytes in some parishes go through the motions and it's clear they have little interest in, or understanding of, their own actions. They've simply been socialized into the "way things are done around here."

The ways of the community must be explained so that apprentices are brought to a place of understanding in which they choose to live according to the truth of the community because they believe it as individuals and not merely because it's what they've been habituated to do. A good apprentice knows both the what and how of the trade they're learning. The apprentice electrician knows how to strip the wire and flip the breakers, but that apprentice also has been brought to understand the reasons and theory behind why they're to strip the wire and flip the breakers the way they do. The same can happen for young Christians who not only watch baptism but also are brought to understand the reasons behind it.

As a result, a well-employed community of faith approach does not reject all forms of instruction, but rather instruction becomes a formational method used toward the goal of developing young people amidst the lives of the community. This means that teenagers receive the same instruction as the rest of the congregation, although handholds and helps might be provided to assist them in understanding the instruction at a developmentally appropriate level.

> **Instruction as an educational method used within a community of faith approach would best happen embedded in the life of the community rather than in an age-based classroom.**

The following case study for using instruction as a method within the community of faith approach comes from Woodland Presbyterian Church in Philadelphia, Pennsylvania. Some years ago the church adopted a community of faith approach, hoping to see young people and newcomers experience enculturation, or a gradual acquisition of the character and ways of the community. But leaders knew this would happen both through participation in the life and acts of the community and through explanation and understanding of why the community operated as it did.

The primary context for learning and faith formation was intended to be the liturgy and life of the congregation, and so instead of creating a separate class, leaders decided that liturgy was also the most reasonable place for instruction to happen. But they did this creatively by using the slides they projected on the wall as an instruction method to further draw people into the life and ways of the congregation. In small print at the bottom of each slide, they projected a short explanation of the meaning of that portion of the liturgy, why it was performed, and how it fit with the rest of what was happening.

Previously those who attended Woodland's worship services may have wondered why everyone sat silently in the pews without speaking to one another before the beginning of the service. By all accounts, to the average visitor, it appeared that this was a very unfriendly church—until an explanatory slide began helping people understand otherwise:

2

> **Silent Personal Preparation:** Our world is cluttered with noise, so we enter into a time and place of rest, refreshment, and refuge for the weary. Prepare yourself for this time by quieting yourself before the Lord.

The service would then begin with someone standing and giving a call to worship. The projection screen would show congregants the text of the call to worship, but more importantly an explanation about what was happening appeared in small print at the bottom:

> **Call to Worship:** The people are called to enter into God's presence. We worship in response to God's call. True worship comes as a result of divine initiative, not human striving.

Throughout the liturgy the slides continued to reveal the meaning behind each aspect and even the reason for the order of the various liturgical elements. Why did the passing of the peace always follow the confession of sin and assurance of God's pardon? Suddenly the slides revealed why:

> **Passing the Peace:** Having been reconciled to God, we now greet each other with the peace of Christ. With extended arms the leader says, "The peace of Christ be with you." The people respond with open arms, "And also with you." We then greet other congregants with, "The peace of Christ be with you."

After a few weeks the regulars stopped noticing these explanations tucked at the bottom of the projected slides, but for newer members of the community, these explanations were a vital source of meaning as they became enfolded into the rhythms of the community.

Rather than starting with an instructional goal and creating a separate class for teenagers or newcomers to learn about the liturgy and its meaning for their lives, Woodland Presbyterian decided to use instruction as a method toward their larger goal of bringing people more fully into the richness of the faith.

Taking this approach to guiding youth in faith and teaching the Bible can sometimes feel daunting to young youth workers because it often requires the coordination of various leaders and elements within the congregation. The payoff, however, can be immense as you and other leaders watch youth become immersed in the life of the community while learning what it actually means to live as Christians.

. . . .

When Jeremy reached the end of the chapter, his coffee cup was empty, but his head was full and buzzing with the ideas described in Seymour's book. Pretty much everything he'd read had caught him off guard. He'd spent the past week immersed in understanding the rhythms of the instructional approach, and he had been amazed at the engaged response of his Sunday school class to the prodigal son lesson. *Go instructional approach!* he had thought at the time. But now he was being forced to rethink everything.

He wondered if part of the problem he'd encountered with Sunday school all these months was that he was trying to impart faith in the contrived environment of the classroom. It had always bothered him how separated teenagers were from the rest of the congregation. While Oak Harbor Church offered two worship services, most youth came with their parents only during the second service and had to choose between Sunday school or "big church."

While Jeremy knew that youth Sunday school wasn't gaining any fans, he also realized that most teenagers who sat through the worship service felt bored and alienated. "I've heard it all before in Sunday school, but in big church I have no idea what I'm hearing," a ninth grader had recently told him. What he'd just read about sanctuary-based youth ministry was compelling, but comments such as that made Jeremy skeptical. With so much going on in his head, he decided to drop by Oak Harbor Assisted Living and bounce a few questions and ideas off Seymour.

. . . .

"I didn't expect to see you so soon, but it seems the chapter on the community of faith has gotten to you," Seymour said delightedly, after Jeremy had recounted his thoughts and questions. "So you've said a lot about how ineffective you think 'big church' is for forming the faith of teenagers, and yet you're also questioning whether the classroom is effective. Both of those are questions of context: What's the right context for studying the Bible with teens, for forming them in faith, and so forth? However, I think the question you have to ask first is the Holy Spirit question."

"The Holy Spirit question?" Jeremy asked puzzled.

"Jeremy! Yes, the Holy Spirit question! My, oh, my. We've talked about this one: How do you believe the Holy Spirit is at work?" Seymour asked while eyeing him.

"Oh, yes, *that* Holy Spirit question, right." Jeremy responded, feeling stupid for having forgotten one of Seymour's most favorite talking points.

Seymour went on to say: "If you believe that one of the normal ways for people to encounter the work of the Holy Spirit is through the historic practices of the Christian faith, then the answer is clear: Our role is to put young people in touch with those practices through which they're likely to experience that mediated grace. Do you believe that's one way the Holy Spirit works?"

"So, if I say yes, are you going to tell me I should shut down Sunday school and move all teenagers into the sanctuary?" Jeremy asked with a sudden twinge of delight. He wondered if Seymour was about to deliver the atom bomb of youth ministry, allowing him to put an end to the battle over Sunday school once and for all.

"Not at all," Seymour responded. "You've got to stop thinking with this either-or mentality. If you believe that the Holy Spirit mediates grace through the practices and life of the community, then it would make sense for you to ensure that teenagers are involved in some form or fashion. And that's a separate question from whether the Holy Spirit can also work through instructional classroom lessons."

Jeremy thought for a moment, pondering the times in his life when he remembered experiencing God or feeling like he had been touched by God's grace. And, if he was honest, some of those experiences happened in the liturgy, in receiving Communion, and in his own baptism when he was seventeen. "I think I do believe that grace can be mediated to teenagers through the practices of the community," he told Seymour. "I'm just not convinced it happens often enough."

"Ah, but is the problem that the Holy Spirit doesn't show up enough, or that we don't prepare young people to be receptive and aware of the Spirit's work in those times and spaces?" Seymour queried.

The role of the human teacher is to pray and prepare the altar for the transforming grace of the Spirit of Jesus.

Seymour continued, "Maybe we haven't been building that altar well."

"Maybe," Jeremy said. "But can you help me think through how I might try using a community of faith approach? I mean, I have no idea what to do."

Jeremy and Seymour spent the afternoon brainstorming an attempt at engaging the youth of Oak Harbor in a new way. Seymour suggested Jeremy ground the entire learning experience in the story of the prodigal son. "But that was last week," Jeremy protested.

"But you only mined a small amount of the meaning and power of that text for the lives of teenagers," Seymour retorted. "That passage is plenty rich for a second week of exploration." He suggested that Jeremy talk to Pastor Jack about moving youth from the classroom into the worship service on an upcoming Sunday in which the liturgy would be focused on the story from Luke 15. After a few text messages, Jack agreed and volunteered to preach on the passage even though it deviated from his usual use of the lectionary. Seymour suggested they find ways to ensure that the liturgy be infused with symbolism drawn from the prodigal son story and find ways to involve teenagers in legitimate, peripheral participation during the service. Within 90 minutes they had created the plan for an intergenerational worship experience that also functioned to open the Bible to teenagers (and adults) in unique ways.

. . . .

"Why are we going into big church?" Brooke, a precocious eighth-grader queried, as Jeremy corralled students out of the youth room and toward the sanctuary.

"We're trying something different; learning in a new way, hopefully," he responded. "And we're looking at the prodigal son again, because there's still a lot to learn there."

The service was about to begin as they entered the sanctuary. Images of the prodigal son as portrayed in paintings and other art rotated in succession on the overhead screen, subtly preparing the congregation for the theme of the morning. As they sang an opening hymn, Jeremy wondered how many people noticed the words contained veiled references to the prodigal son story. And when they transitioned to a more contemporary song, "Forever

Reign," he wondered the same while singing the words in the refrain, "I'm running to your arms."

The Scripture for the morning was, of course, Luke 15:11-32, and it was read expertly by a high school student. The prayer of confession, led by an adult congregant, was written to connect to the prodigal son story by focusing on ways that Christians run away from God and squander God's gifts. "Father, we have sinned against heaven and against you," the congregation prayed in unison echoing the words of Luke 15. The assurance of pardon, offered by a middle school student, promised that forgiveness has been secured and spoke of a warm welcome by the God who embraces wayward children. As the liturgy moved to the passing of the peace, the congregation was invited to greet one another with a similar open embrace.

Pastor Jack's sermon focused on ways Christians often run from the Heavenly Father and then believe they won't be welcomed back. It was followed by two testimonies Jeremy had arranged. Larry, a member of the congregation in his mid-50s, spoke about God's help in getting his life back together after losing his job and family because of his addiction to pain medication. "I definitely was the younger brother who ran away and couldn't find my way back. And I didn't believe God would take me back—but I was wrong," Larry testified.

The second testimony was even more powerful as Larry's college-aged daughter spoke about her struggles to accept God's grace for her father. "I wanted to be like the older brother, refusing to accept God's grace for my dad or to show any grace myself because he'd hurt us so much," she shared. "But after my own struggles in life, I ultimately had to acknowledge and accept that we're all the younger brother in need of grace."

They closed the service by celebrating the Lord's Supper. Pastor Jack reminded the congregation: "Communion is about God saying to each of us, 'Welcome home, let us eat together; this child of mine was dead and has come back to life!' When we partake of the blood and body of Christ, we are reminded that we have been welcomed back into the arms of God, not as servants but as God's own children."

As congregants departed the sanctuary, ushers distributed a family discussion guide that included questions for use in continuing their reflection on the prodigal son story at home over lunch.

Pastor Jack cornered Jeremy after the service and said: "This was a very good experience, and I'm glad you had the idea. I've heard great things from some of our older members; they really enjoyed the richness of the service this morning. Do you think the youth benefited from it?"

"Well, they seemed decently attentive," Jeremy said. "It's just hard to know after doing something like this one time. But I do think they benefited from engaging with the whole congregation and seeing their peers involved in the liturgy. You see," Jeremy explained, "it's not the goal of this teaching approach to learn one big point about the biblical text, but rather for youth to learn the rhythms of faith week in and week out amidst the community of faith."

"It makes me happy to hear you say that. It means you learned something," came a familiar voice from behind Jeremy. He turned around to find Seymour sauntering at a slow pace down the sanctuary aisle. While the old man seemed to move with agility in the confines of his small apartment, here in the open expanse of the church Jeremy could see why Seymour had difficulty getting out much.

"I wasn't going to miss this for anything," Seymour continued, "and it didn't disappoint—except for that song about running into your arms or whatever. I don't think I'll be running anywhere to anyone anytime soon."

Jack and Jeremy chuckled as Seymour took a seat in one of the pews to rest. "And this is for you," Seymour said, digging a folded piece of paper out of his pocket and handing it to Jeremy.

"What is it?" Jeremy asked puzzled.

"Your next reading assignment, of course," Seymour replied with a grin.

Download the full leader's guide for Jeremy's community of faith approach lesson on the prodigal son, including all liturgical elements, by *visiting http://www.youthministrypartners.com/tob*.

Endnotes

[1] Discussed in "The One-Eared Mickey Mouse," by Stuart Cummings-Bond, in *Youth Worker Journal,* Fall, 1989; pages 76-78.

[2] For more information see *Almost Christian: What the Faith of Our Teenagers Is Telling the American Church*, by Kenda Creasy Dean (Oxford University Press, Inc., 2010).

CHAPTER 3: THE INTERPRETIVE APPROACH

I tried to read it," Jeremy explained to Seymour the next week when they met again. Seymour had assigned Jeremy chapter 3 in the blue book to read before their meeting. "Really, I tried. Honestly, I couldn't understand very much of it at all," he told the elderly man. Seymour looked at him incredulously. "No, really," Jeremy pleaded. "I gave it 20 minutes, but all the philosophical and psychological stuff was too much. I just couldn't follow it."

"That's fine," Seymour responded calmly, not tipping his hand at his displeasure. He then thought for a long moment before speaking. "I think I have a way to explain it to you. Come and take a look at this," he said, while pulling an iPad from the magazine rack beside his chair. Jeremy was surprised Seymour had an iPad; he was even more surprised he knew how to use it.

"You know," Seymour said with a bit of wonder in his voice, "I find YouTube so amazing; oh, the things you can find on there." Before Jeremy even knew what was happening, Seymour had pulled up the site, searched for the clip he wanted, and hit play. "Just watch," Seymour instructed.

Jeremy watched as two crudely drawn triangles moved around the screen in a poorly animated video. The two triangles, one bigger and one smaller, collided, and then went spinning off together.

Jeremy assumed the larger triangle was trying to push the smaller out the door of a square that appeared to be their home. Then the screen went black.

"What in the world was that?" Jeremy asked with a flummoxed expression. "I need to send you better links for some videos worth watching."

Ignoring Jeremy's comments, Seymour pressed on, "So the question is, what are the triangles doing?"

"Well, honestly, I'd say the big one was the mommy triangle and the smaller one was the baby triangle," Jeremy said with a laugh. "And there were certain things the little triangle was ready to do, such as spinning and dancing; but he wasn't ready to be pushed out of the nest."

Seymour raised an eyebrow and stared at Jeremy for a moment. "Interesting," Seymour deadpanned.

"Why? Did I get it wrong?" Jeremy asked. "What was I supposed to see? What are the triangles actually doing?"

"They're simply moving, Jeremy. Any interpretation of what they're doing and their motivation, as well as any relationship, must be supplied by the viewer. There are many different interpretations of what's happening there, but the point is that the triangles are simply shapes moving around a screen. Yet, you had an innate, automatic inclination to provide a narrative for the triangles and to interpret their movement by telling a meaningful story. And the way you did that was by employing your imagination. That's a good thing, and it's part of what it means to be human."

Jeremy was still stuck on the triangles, convinced that Seymour was wrong and that the big triangle was certainly the parent. Seymour continued, "The great philosopher Paul Ricoeur once said, 'A life is no more than a biological phenomenon as long as it is not interpreted.' In other words, unless some kind of meaning is imparted to the succession of life events, then it is nothing more than a series of birth, breaths, and death. Life is just a succession of meaningless events—until it's interpreted. We're the ones who mentally configure life into something meaningful through the act of interpretation. So, maybe the goal of Christian formation and opening the Bible with teenagers should be to help teenagers interpret the world and their lives and make meaning of it all. Someone is going to help them interpret these things, so why shouldn't it be the church? Yet too often it's not us, because the church has primarily been interested in giving them Bible knowledge instead of giving them an ideology."

"An ideology?" Jeremy asked, suddenly alarmed by Seymour's strange choice of words. "The last thing I want is to indoctrinate kids with an ideology!"

"You're taking too negative a view on my use of the word *ideology*," said Seymour. "I'm using it the way Erik Erikson talked about ideology—as one of the things that secures a person's identity. A way of making sense of the world. Everyone has an ideology from which they must operate if they're going to make any sense of the world, and it's usually derived from the community we embrace."[1]

Seymour continued, "For example, I was listening to a radio interview this morning about a wealthy billionaire who truly believes that humans are not equal in fundamental worth, dignity, and value; rather he believes the value of any life is determined by how much wealth the person controls."

"What? That's crazy! I can't believe someone would say that," said Jeremy.

"Is it?" responded Seymour. "It actually makes a lot of sense."

"No, it doesn't make sense," Jeremy interrupted, perplexed by Seymour's sudden defense of such an onerous idea. "This goes against everything Jesus was about; it goes against the idea that our value stems from being created in the image of God. I mean, tangible wealth doesn't last beyond this world but, through the grace of God, human life continues!"

"Ah, very good," said Seymour with a wry smile. "Quite the impassioned defense—of an ideology—of a particular way of giving meaning to the world that is based out of belief given to you by a surrounding community."

> **Any ideology is a particular system of ideas and ideals that helps us see the world and understand our role in it. It's basically the story out of which each of us lives.**

Seymour continued: "Your offense at the billionaire's notion arises from the way in which your ideology contrasts sharply with his. Humans are storytellers, but we don't just tell stories. We live by them."

Jeremy mulled this over. "But what does that even mean, that we live by a story?" he queried. "Isn't that taking a story too seriously? I mean, a story is just a story."

"Oh, no, no, no!" Seymour was on the edge of his seat now, excited and shaking a bit. Jeremy was nervous that he'd fall right out of the chair onto the floor. But Seymour continued: "Stories orient us to what is true, what is beautiful, what is good, what is worthwhile. Stories tell us where we come from, where we're going, and how we'll know when we get there. It's stories that tell us how we should live. Most powerfully, stories tell us who we are. In fact, not too long ago I remember reading about a study that discovered that minorities often believe the cultural story and stereotypes told about them to such a degree that, on standardized tests where they had to indicate their race, their scores dropped. Stories are serious business!"

Seymour finally sat back in his seat, and Jeremy breathed a sigh of relief that he wouldn't be tending the old man's broken hip anytime soon. "You see, Jeremy," Seymour continued at a slower pace, "life . . . well, life is a story. And telling a story is impossible unless you impart particular meaning to things and give certain details weight and importance that other events don't have. Since there are many ways to tell a story, there are many ways to understand the meaning of your life:

- What are your defining moments?
- What role do you play in the story: the hero, the coward, the successful one, the failure?
- And what is your story all about in the end? Is it about getting rich? being a person who gives back? being a great spouse and parent?
- And what's on the final page of your story?

"Our final story hasn't been written yet, but all of us have an idea of the direction and a certain hope about where our lives and stories are headed," Seymour said.

"I think I understand your point about stories, but what does this have to do with the ideology stuff you were just talking about, and why does any of this matter for teaching?" Jeremy asked bewildered.

"Let me try to put it together simply: What if the ideology, the system of belief about the world and yourself, most usually comes in the form of a story? Your story of who you are is always with you, residing just beneath the surface, and the story you believe about your life—what it means and where it's headed—guides and helps determine your choices, how you live and what you do, because it tells you who you are."

"OK, and the teaching part, this matters to teaching because . . . ?" Jeremy trailed off and began listening to Seymour explain.

3

A DEEPER LEVEL OF TRANSFORMATION

Since a system of belief about the world and yourself most usually comes in the form of a story, teaching becomes a matter of helping young people interpret the meaning of their individual lives and their attitude and approach to the world through the story of Christ. What if the stories of the Bible help to orient teenagers' own self-conception and their approach and attitude to the world? It's a level of transformation that is far deeper than simply finding an application point in Scripture. This is the aim of another system of teaching called the interpretive approach.

Teaching teenagers the facts and the content of the Bible is very important. The *instructional approach* imparts knowledge and understanding that students apply to their lives. However, the *interpretive approach* is more concerned with seeing youth interpret their lives through the lens of God's story, and thereby come to live out of a different view of self.

Those who take the interpretive approach would argue that the change in lifestyle that accompanies a traditional instructional lesson is a matter of simply modifying discrete behaviors; but the interpretive approach aims at changing the totality of the lived experience of the student.

> **The instructional approach is about transferring principles
> into the teenager's world. The interpretive method is about
> transferring the teenager into the world of the scriptural narrative.**

So what does it mean to transfer people into the scriptural narrative? Think of it this way: Madeleine L'Engle, the author best known for *A Wrinkle in Time*, was herself a devout Christian and actually wrote quite a few biblical fiction books. One of those books, *Many Waters*, followed two of the characters from *A Wrinkle in Time* on a sort of mind-bending, time-travel adventure in which

3

they end up setting down in the age of Noah. They run into Noah and his family who are busy building the ark. The twin boys at the center of the story are deeply impacted by their encounter with an entire community whom they realize will soon be destroyed by the Flood. They know that only Noah and his family will be saved. By the end of the book, these boys quite literally have been transformed in their perspectives, outlooks, and ways of life by entering the biblical narrative.

While *Many Waters* is fiction, and a person cannot of course time travel to help Noah build the ark, youth workers who take an interpretive approach want to find ways for young people to truly enter the story or be captivated by the story. They don't want teenagers to just hear the story, but rather actually experience the story so that their individual lives are changed by the story as it comes to define them differently.

Imagination is key. In her book, *The God-Hungry Imagination*, Christian educator and youth worker Sarah Arthur recalls the conversion of C.S. Lewis from an atheistic teenager to one of the greatest Christian voices of the twentieth century. Was Lewis converted by rational arguments for the existence and presence of God? Far from it. Instead, Lewis read a fantasy novel by minister and author George MacDonald and said that it converted and "baptized his imagination!"[2]

"Baptized his imagination" is not just a throwaway line. Fantasy fiction draws us into a world that operates differently from our own. Many of the contours and details of the fantasy worlds we read about are familiar, yet every fantasy novel makes subtle (or sometimes not so subtle) twists on how the world works and what is expected. Different values, ethics, and ways of living one's life are exposed in great detail. We don't just enter the story, but we enter an alternative way of experiencing and interpreting the very meaning of life.

When we finish the novel, or the movie ends, we are released back into our own world, and yet we return with a different way of seeing our living existence and what it means in light of the use of imagination. So, for Lewis to talk about a baptized imagination, he's speaking of imagining the world through the eyes of Christian faith.

> **At the heart of the interpretive approach is an invitation to imagine our world and our experiences in a Christian framework and to see the meaning of it from a different perspective.**

Such imagination can impart to youth a different ideology, a different interpretation out of which they can live.

IMAGINATION AS THE DOMAIN OF THE HOLY SPIRIT

But what's so powerful about imagination? Why should we think that's the magic bullet? Actually, imagination isn't the magic bullet. But, imagination matters because one of the ways the Holy Spirit works is through our God-given imaginative processes. The instructional approach urges us to examine the meaning of every word, phrase, and metaphor in Scripture so that we can bring students to rational understanding of the Bible. Meanwhile those who take an interpretive approach say that the Holy Spirit slips "unnoticed through the back door of imagination."[3] That's Sarah Arthur's way of explaining that the Holy Spirit can be at work when we imagine and that our role as teachers is to bring students into experiences where the Holy Spirit can woo and transform our imagination.

Arthur is keen to point out that she's not alone in her belief: Old Testament scholar Ellen Davis says "the human faculty that has the greatest potential for connecting us with God" is the imagination.[4]

And theologian Garrett Green has pointed to imagination as the "point of contact for divine revelation."[5]

At its most basic, imagination is the ability to see and experience things that can't be seen with the eyes, and the Spirit enlivens and quickens our imagination to see all of existence through the eyes and mind of Christ.

In the instructional approach, it is primarily the action and words of the teacher who knows the language and culture well that can bring the student to understand the ancient words of Scripture. But in the interpretive approach, there is a belief that the Holy Spirit is the one who transforms meaning by working through the imagination, and there is a trust that the Spirit will "do far beyond all that we could ask or imagine by his power at work within us" (Ephesians 3:20).

Therefore, we do not always need carefully crafted outcomes for our lessons or need to know exactly where the discussion will lead. Rather, the role of the human teacher is to lead youth to use their imagination in engaging the story of God in hopes of the young person making meaningful connections between the Scripture, the world, and her life.[6] However, it is the Holy Spirit who knits together the disparate parts of life through imagination and is a creative force, making and exposing connections where none seemed to exist before.

IMAGINATION AND IMPLICATION

"I think I get it," Jeremy intoned, "but I have no idea how I'd go about helping teenagers interpret their lives by imaginatively entering the biblical story. I'm trying to think how this works. So, let's start at the beginning: How would I go about opening up Genesis 1, for example, and teach that God created the world while helping students interpret their lives? I'm at a loss."

"Let's walk through this together," said Seymour. "In this case, we want teenagers to interpret their lives through the lens of the Creation narrative. So it's not enough to say 'God created the world' and teach that as a point of knowledge. Rather, we want them to consider what this means for how they view the world and for the meaning they make in their own lives. We can't necessarily control the meaning that students form, but we should have at least some good ideas of the trajectory of meaning before we go down the path.

"So what does it mean to say we believe that God created the world? One thing it means is that we live in a universe of order and intention. All things have the potential to be good, beautiful, and true because they were originally ordered by a God of goodness, beauty, and truth. Having such a perspective gives one a very different imagination with which to approach the world than if we start with a naturalistic view of the universe in which there is no creator at all.

"Second, one of the beautiful things about the Creation narrative, I've always thought, is that God invites humanity to cooperate in the creation. There are aspects of creation that God gives to people, such as the naming of the animals. Humans stand out as cocreators with God of a universe teeming with possibility. When the Creation narrative opens, there is nothing but darkness, chaos, and the abyss. God seeds the universe with truth, goodness, and beauty and brings forth order, light, and life. And astoundingly, God ordains humans as gardeners of possibility who are called by God to bring forth the fruits of truth, goodness, and beauty into the world."

Listening intently as the old man continued to speak, Jeremy found himself awed by Seymour's sudden eloquence on the meaning of Creation.

ordered intentions of God. And then Novelli, with a second simple question makes a turn that clearly separates what he's doing from usual instructional methods; he asks, 'What does it mean for you personally to be created in this God's image?'"

Seymour paused a moment to let the question hang in the air, then said: "When you think about that question, what's powerful is that students are drawn in to imagine the nature of God. And because of their imagining—because of them artfully turning it over in their heads in the Spirit's domain of imagination—they're able to consider a whole new meaning for their lives as those created in the image of God. They might be able to see their own lives caught up in divine purpose."

> **Through imagining and the work of the Spirit, the reality of Creation moves beyond mere trivia to something that potentially awakens teenagers to the meaning of Creation and grounds all of life and their self-conceptions in a created order.**

"Maybe …," Jeremy said with an air of skepticism, "that might happen for some, but certainly not all teenagers. I have a squirrelly group of boys who would fall asleep during the reading of the story long before God gets to the seventh day."

"Oh, Jeremy, that's true regardless of the approach or method. Any one teaching moment is going to be effective for some students but not others. The point is continually helping students the best we can to be ready for the quickening grace of the Holy Spirit. As I've said before, those who use an interpretive approach believe one of the best ways to do that is to lead students into imagining, but that doesn't always happen through an immersive story experience."

"What are the essentials if I'm going to try teaching with an interpretive approach?" Jeremy asked. "And let's assume I don't want to try this immersive storying kind of thing."

Taking advantage of Jeremy's attention, Seymour continued: "So, our task is to open youth to imagining their lives, their actions, and their world within a creation framework that God has seeded with possibilities for goodness. One way of doing this is using a Bible storying method that invites young people to imagine their world and their lives differently by asking questions that require students to literally put themselves in the story."[7]

"The goal isn't application, but rather implication, or the desire to see students bound up with or folded in with the story. The hope is they begin to find meaning for their lives through the story, rather than just figuring out what to do with the story."[8]

> **This can be accomplished through an artful retelling of the Creation narrative with rich imagery that draws students to focus on the acts of God as they're invited to listen and imagine the story.**

"Are you trying to tell me the interpretive approach is just about being a good storyteller?" Jeremy asked incredulously.

"No, not at all!" Seymour quickly said. "The artful narrative isn't why the method is powerful, but once students are drawn in to the imagining, usually the story is followed up with 'wondering questions' that get them thinking and imagining deeply about the story. I've seen this done using the Creation narrative by of the originators of the method, Michael Novelli, and the s power of the method has been realized with just two questi First, he asks, 'What do you notice about God in the story brings listeners to focus on the character and actions of a brings order out of chaos and goodness and light out of and the abyss. Some listeners would notice the gentlene others the loving kindness of God, and still others the

PARTS TO AN INTERPRETIVE APPROACH

"I'd say there are three essential steps to the interpretive approach," explained Seymour:

- First, you have to **accept** and invite to the table the students' individual experiences and ways of seeing the meaning of their lives and the world. This acceptance of experiences is crucial for creating a climate of trust that can allow imagination to happen.

- Second, we invite students into imagining a different kind of world, the biblical world that is informed by the Christian narrative. Into this world they bring their ways of seeing and understanding, and so we must help them **imagine** a world that is different and in which they notice values, systems, meanings, and ways of life that undergird this alternative world and are distinct from their own. This can happen through the richness of a storying method, but story is not actually the key; any method works as long as it engages them to imagine life framed by a different set of values and ways of perceiving the world.

- Third, it must **release** them back into their own existence to imagine how the new ways of perceiving and giving meaning to the world gained through imagination change how they understand their personal lives and the world around them. They must imagine how their personal lives and experience are "re-meaned" by this new way of seeing the world.

"Let me give you an example drawn from an activity I used with groups of teenage boys back when I was much, much younger. I would construct between two trees a life-size spider's web using clothesline, and I would make the holes of the web just large enough for a body to pass through. The holes were of varying sizes since people come in various sizes. I would assign the group the task of getting everyone from one side of the spider's web to the other by going through the holes in the web—but each hole could only be used one time. Once a person had passed through a hole, it was ineligible for reuse by another.

"Now, you may have seen or heard of such an activity being used as a team-building exercise. But that wasn't my goal in this case. I wanted to use the experience as the framework for an interpretive approach Bible lesson. So, I'd take the group of boys to the spider's web, give them instructions and, just to add to the drama and competition, I'd set a timer and tell them the previous group took just 12 minutes or so. 'Surely, YOU can do better,' I'd goad them. And then I'd stand back and watch the chaos unfold.

"There was always a boy who would immediately pick his hole and jump through it, leaving the rest of the group to fend for themselves. Invariably a few boys would vie for leadership, trying to one-up the other's expertise and weight with the group. A few would offer up solutions to the puzzle, but when drowned out by the other boys, would withdraw from the game and sit on a nearby stump. Still others were bossed around by the more dominant guys and would become incredibly frustrated at being pulled in this or that direction. Usually 12 minutes is all it took for the group to devolve into anger, frustration, factions, and general mayhem.

"At that point, I'd call a time out and reassemble them sitting in a circle. Everything that had transpired to this point was actually preparing them for opening the Bible using the interpretive approach.

"First, I would take some time and go around the circle asking each boy what he thought about the previous experience and what he thought had gone wrong with the group. The rest of the group was instructed to remain silent as each boy spoke, expressing his interpretation of the experience without insult, pushback, or comment from the others.

"Then, moving into the second step of the interpretive process, I invited them into imagining a different kind of world and a different form of relating to one another. I read aloud 1 Corinthians 12, usually twice, and then asked them to imagine a group of people who live and act like the body of Christ that Paul describes. I would ask questions such as:

- What holds that group together?
- What motivates them?
- Why do they clothe the dishonorable parts with honor rather than just kicking them out?

"Third, I would draw the boys back into our present experience by asking questions like:

- If we lived and acted like the body of Christ while in this spider's web activity, how would you act differently from the way you acted a few moments ago?
- How does understanding yourself as a member of the body of Christ change your view about the goal of this game and your role in it?
- How does it change the way you understand your responsibility toward every other member of the group?

"Notice that the boys had been asked to imagine a different world in the second step, but here they were transferring the meaning of that world into their experience in the present world.

"Finally, with a new way of seeing themselves individually and collectively firmly in place, I would release them to try the game again, approaching it from a 1 Corinthians perspective. Sometimes there was still tension, but the change in their approach to the game and one another was palpable. It was amazing to watch them embody kindness, care, and deference toward one another as they worked together to solve the challenge."

"That's fascinating and a cool way to use that game but I don't see how that's an interpretive approach," Jeremy admitted. "Where was the storying aspect you've talked about so much?"

"Don't get hung up looking for an immersive story," Seymour cautioned. "Look for the places an interpretive lesson draws students to imagine a different kind of world, one shaped by Christian meaning. While the reading of 1 Corinthians 12 didn't strike your ears as story, it did draw them into imagining a different order to life. By asking them questions and considering how and why the body of Christ might function the way Paul describes, they were engaged in imagination. Further, we imagined what being the body of Christ might look like in our circumstances."

Storying, however flowery or bare bones, is merely a gateway to imagination.

Intrigued by his discussion with Seymour, especially the opportunity to engage students imaginatively in youth ministry, Jeremy decided he'd try his hand at operating out of the interpretive approach. "Do you think it would be OK if I tried the prodigal son story yet again with my students next Sunday?" he asked Seymour cautiously. "I mean, the biggest complaint I always get is that they've heard it all before. I've presented them with this same Scripture passage twice and I'm proposing a third time. Talk about the definition of 'heard it all before.'"

"I think it's a fine idea," Seymour responded without hesitation. "They've heard the story, but have they entered into it imaginatively in a search for meaning? Doubtful. So if you do it well, my guess is it will feel like a whole new story to them. Definitely give it a try."

. . . .

Jeremy thought about Seymour's three suggested components of the interpretive approach: *Accept*, *Imagine*, and *Release* were the words he wrote in his notes:

- **Accept** the experience and meaning of the student.

- **Imagine** with them a world that operates on kingdom values.

- **Release** them back into their own world to see the meaning of their lives differently.

For a long time he pondered what this could look like with the prodigal son story. Prompting students to think about and share their experiences of forgiveness would be a productive way to begin the lesson: "Tell about a time you were forgiven for something you did wrong. How did it make you feel? Now tell about a time you were challenged to forgive; was it difficult? What did you end up doing?" Beyond that he was stumped. He wanted to help students imagine, but he had concerns as he thought about actually doing this with the teenagers in his group. He decided to give Seymour a call.

"Here's my problem," began Jeremy. "I can get them imagining and entering the story, but these kids have no idea what it's like to have lived in first-century Palestine!" complained Jeremy as Seymour listened intently on the phone. "The world of the characters in the story is totally different from the world of Oak Harbor. My youth have no reference point from which to do anything but transpose their personal experience in twenty-first-century America into the text. So I'm stumped as to how to get them imagining."

"Jeremy, you're missing the point," Seymour said. "Imagining with historical accuracy isn't the goal. Imagination is the locus of the Spirit, and we want them to imagine life lived by a very different set of values and principles, by the kingdom values of the God revealed in Scripture. Besides, the characters in the prodigal son story didn't live in first-century Palestine. It's a parable. These characters were imagined by Jesus himself. The historical details aren't as important as focusing on the ways the characters act in relationships. I think your role in helping them imagine is to give them enough detail to allow them to see how the father's actions and the father's heart contrast sharply with the actions and values we might expect.

"You know," Seymour continued, "it reminds me a bit of the ancient Greeks who used epic stories to educate. In fact, at one point in Greek history, to be educated meant memorizing the *Odyssey* and the *Iliad*, Homer's great imaginative works. To say you were 'cultured' as a Greek meant to drink so deeply from the well of those stories that you couldn't just imagine the actions of Odysseus or Achilles recorded in the story, but you could imagine what they would do in your shoes and in your situation. In other words, to be cultured meant to have your imagination and your personal story formed by the stories that gripped the psyche of all good Greeks. I think the interpretive approach is aiming for something similar to happen for students through the story of God. In this case, how does it affect students if they imagine what the prodigal's father would do if placed into the situations of life they face?"

Jeremy thought about this for a moment, then said: "I think that's great, but I wonder if the story is so familiar at this point that they won't see what's unusual. It no longer strikes them as odd or amazing that the father welcomes back the son with open arms. So what if I first have them imagine how the story should have gone based on the values and normal ways of the world around us? Maybe I have them imagine different responses that the father *could* have had to the prodigal before imagining how the father *did* respond in the story, followed up by how the father might respond in the situations we face in life today. What do you think?"

"That is certainly worth trying," Seymour responded. "Sometimes the only way to know is to try. The important thing is this: intentionality. You're intentionally thinking through how to best open the Bible with teenagers by attending to the ways you believe the Holy Spirit works in our lives. Your ideas are not always going to work as you hope, but that's OK. Remember, the Holy Spirit is The Teacher. The best you can do, like Elijah, is to faithfully prepare the altar and the firewood and pray for the work of God."

"Wait a second," Jeremy interrupted. "I didn't realize it until now, but I used a similar kind of imagining in the instructional lesson I wrote on this passage. I asked the students to write and perform skits that imagined the thoughts and actions of the older brother. Now I'm asking them to imagine things from the perspective of the father. How can I call that first lesson instructional but say this one is crafted in the interpretive approach? I think I messed up."

Seymour quickly reminded Jeremy:

Teaching is not defined by the method used but by the goal toward which it aims.

"Yes, the skit activity required students to imagine," said Seymour, "but as I said at the time, we used that activity for the purpose of moving students toward understanding and application. But in this interpretive approach lesson, you're hoping to use imagination to gift them with a new meaning and vision that guides the way they look at their identity."

When Jeremy hung up the phone he had a better sense of where to go with the lesson and developed a complete teaching plan. But when he walked into class on Sunday, he decided to use only a simple outline that summarized the session:

ACCEPT: The experience and meaning of the student

- Tell about a time you were forgiven; how did it make you feel?

- Tell about a time you were challenged to forgive; was it difficult, and what did you end up doing?

IMAGINE: Operating with the heart of the father

- Imagine together different ways the father could have responded to the prodigal son's return.

- Now, as I read aloud the story, imagine yourself in the father's place; what do you feel at each point along the way?

RELEASE: Back to their world to see their lives differently

- If the father in this story were standing next to you in some of the situations in your life when you've required forgiveness, what do you imagine he would whisper in your ear?

- How do you think differently about yourself and your responsibility knowing that you're a child of the God who forgives like the father in this story?

Download the full leader's guide for Jeremy's interpretive approach lesson on the prodigal son by visiting *http://www. youthministrypartners.com/tob*.

Endnotes

[1] The way that Erikson uses *ideology* is similar to the more widespread concept of worldview (German: *Weltanschauung*), and there is plenty of conceptual confusion between the two terms in academic circles. However, *ideology* usually carries more implications for how one acts personally and politically. Additionally, *ideology* is almost always connected with a particular community, which communicates Erikson's point that community and ideology usually come hand in hand. I am aware that both *ideology* and *worldview* come with their own conceptual baggage, and invite the reader to focus on the intent of the passage, not the particular word choice.

[2] Discussed in *The God-Hungry Imagination: The Art of Storytelling for Postmodern Youth Ministry*, by Sarah Arthur (Upper Room, 2007); page 38.

[3] From *God-Hungry Imagination*; page 39.

[4] From *Wondrous Depth: Preaching the Old Testament*, by Ellen F. Davis (Westminster John Knox Press, 2005); page 149.

[5] From *Imagining God: Theology and the Religious Imagination*, by Garrett Green (Wm. B. Eerdmans Publishing Co., 1998); page 40.

[6] Discussed in *God-Hungry Imagination*, Arthur; page 58.

[7] See *Shaped by the Story: Discover the Art of Bible Storying*, by Michael Novelli (Sparkhouse Press, 2013) for the development and full articulation of this method.

[8] See *Shaped by the Story*.

CHAPTER 4: THE LIBERATION APPROACH

The rain had been falling in sheets for days, and it wasn't letting up for the Oak Harbor Autumn BBQ and Volleyball Tournament. Jeremy had inherited the annual event from his predecessor. "But this fall it ain't happening," he said to himself as he looked out the window at the flooded church grounds. He was nearly as deflated as the volleyball bobbing in the water around the picnic area. So he made a few calls and sent a mass text message officially canceling the event.

At the very least this frees up my Saturday, Jeremy thought to himself as he plopped back into his office chair. He checked some movie times and pondered how he might spend the day. Then he noticed Seymour's blue book sitting on the edge of his desk.

"Oh, THAT," he groaned as he remembered Seymour had assigned him yet another chapter to read. That had been several weeks ago, and he'd been avoiding Seymour's frequent phone calls and voice mails asking for a visit and chat. *I've learned three of his approaches; surely three should be enough*, he thought as he dismissed the idea of using his Saturday to read. But then he thought about the way in which he'd encountered students who were excited recently after Sunday school and Wednesday night youth group. It was almost as if Jeremy's own excitement and clarity around his teaching goals had sparked a similar excitement in students. He eyed the book again, and as if saying it aloud made it official, he proposed an agreement to himself: "OK, get some coffee, read Seymour's book, and then you've definitely earned that movie this afternoon."

"Deal," he said aloud again, then grabbed the book and his curriculum binder and headed out the door for Coffee Haven. Within a few minutes he'd found his usual spot and, after a sip of a large triple-shot mocha, he began to read.

. . . .

The Spirit of the Lord is upon me, because the Lord has anointed me. He has sent me to preach good news to the poor, to proclaim release to the prisoners and recovery of sight to the blind, to liberate the oppressed, and to proclaim the year of the Lord's favor. —Luke 4:18-19

4

A liberation approach is rooted in an understanding that the gospel is not just future oriented to a time when Christians will find reward in heaven, nor is it just about individual liberation from sin. Rather, God promises liberation from the temporal effects and limited perspectives that are bound up with sin and show forth in our world in terms of factions, violence, oppression, sexism, ageism, income inequality, and so on. To take a liberation approach to opening the Bible with youth is to take seriously the gospel as a liberating message of the kingdom of God that even now is breaking into our living existence. A liberation approach recognizes that sinfulness extends beyond the human heart and takes root in social structures.

A fallen nature characterizes the condition of individual humans as well as the collective condition of humanity. The principalities and powers of which Scripture speaks are not necessarily some kind of ethereal demonic force, but are visible and real forces at work in our world and are oppressing, dehumanizing, domesticating, and degrading the lives of people who bear the *imago dei*, God's very image.

The liberation approach understands gospel as the proclamation of the reign of God that corrects injustice and oppression. The kingdom of God challenges the social order of treating people as things rather than as people of God. The gospel should bring tangible signs of healing to our present-day world through the efforts of people who call themselves by Jesus' name.

As fallible humans we can become blind to the forces of injustice that lull us into compliance. Yet when Jesus Christ, God Incarnate, breaks through into our world, he begins a process of unmasking the powers that bind, sets the normal expectations on their end, and opens eyes and ears as Christ announces the kingdom of God which operates on principles and values quite contrary to our social norms. Jesus' parables alone illustrate this upending of expectations: The outcasts are invited to be guests at the banquet; the worker hired late receives a full wage; the Samaritan becomes the compassionate hero; the widow and her single coin become the model of generosity. In Jesus' world, those who want to be first shall be last and last shall be first. Those who want to save their lives will lose them, and those who lose them for Christ's sake will find them.

Those who promote a liberation approach would say that Christ would be shocked by today's comfortable and socially acceptable form of religion that calls itself by his name. Could it be that much of youth ministry preaches and practices a Christian faith devoid of challenge to the cultural, political, social, and ecclesial status quo?

UNDERSTANDING THE APPROACH

Far from the individualization and spiritualization of the gospel as a message of personal salvation and self-improvement, the liberation approach seeks to move teenagers beyond merely reading the Bible to awakened action. The goal of the liberation approach is to bring awareness and consciousness of features of our social systems and structures that are contrary to God's ideals. For this reason the approach also can be characterized as an awakening or critical pedagogy approach. The desired outcome is that students will undertake action as partners of God in the world, actions that promote justice, healing, wholeness, and release from oppression.

Those who take a liberation approach are interested in seeing the world transformed. They're happy that the interpretive approach wants young people to make meaning of their lives differently, but unless that leads to freedom, justice, and healing for both young people and the world, then interpretation is merely self-indulgent. "It's real nice that you want youth to understand their lives through the biblical story," they might say, then continue: "I hope that makes them feel good about themselves. But I sure see a lot of young people who supposedly interpret their lives through Christ and don't do a thing to proclaim the in-breaking kingdom of God in real and tangible ways to a dying world."

> **Advocates of a liberation approach see the gospel as a radical message that should open our eyes to injustice, oppression, and hatred.**

When believers embody the gospel, then the church will find itself countering the social norms and oppressive practices of the surrounding culture.

A liberation approach is an appropriate name for what is also called critical pedagogy, because the goal is that students' minds are liberated to understand the world differently through new eyes. Further, students are liberated from inaction and disenfranchisement as they come to understand themselves as agents and actors who are able to effect change in the world in partnership with God.

Awareness

A liberation approach is rooted in awareness. The dehumanizing structures that pull us away from faith and dependence and make us complicit with forms of oppression are structures and constructions of which we are largely unaware. We tend to accept the status quo of society without questioning and adopt the interpretive lenses and suppositions of our culture without reflecting on these very "ways of seeing" in light of the gospel.

For example, the way we tend to view gender roles, or even read the Bible's account of gender, tends to be heavily influenced by particular culturally influenced ways of conceiving of men and women. A liberation approach seeks to help students step back and see the ways in which our conceptions of the ideal man or woman are constructions which may dehumanize or oppress others. While an instructional lesson on money might focus on helping youth understand and apply God's intent for giving and generosity, a liberation approach would likely focus on exposing the American cultural value of "getting the best deal" and expose how our pursuit of this cultural value through our love of rolled-back prices at a discount store results in the oppression of impoverished workers around the world.[1]

A liberation approach seeks to move youth to meaningful action.

Meaningful Action

Far from the trivial actions in which youth are often engaged (fun, games, fund raisers, youth group), we should look to involve youth in actions that uncover injustice, seek justice, that are public, and that give youth true voice and value.[2] In such a way, the gospel penetrates their lives but also becomes actualized in our world through the transformative efforts of teenagers.

4

Further, it invites youth to not merely hear and accept the gospel of "recovery of sight for the blind" but also to participate and help "proclaim the year of the Lord's favor" (Luke 4:18) as we refuse to "be conformed to the patterns of this world" (Romans 12:1).

Awakening Youth

One of the goals of a liberation approach is to awaken youth to the ways in which the surrounding culture (and church culture) seek to domesticate and dehumanize them as adolescents. The very idea of adolescence is seen by many as a social construction that oppresses and dehumanizes young people by foisting upon them social expectations that inform the way that society treats youth and the way they consequently behave.[3] As a sort of self-fulfilling prophecy, the script of adolescence prescribes that youth are self-absorbed, rebellious, peer-oriented, and able to contribute to society only through consumption.[4]

As a result of blind acceptance of this adolescent script in the church, teenagers are alienated from God's call to exert their agency and power in the world because we believe they're naturally self-interested and not responsible for the common good. They are alienated from the intergenerational faith community and networks of care because we program youth ministry to be peer focused. Finally, they are alienated from significant social roles within the congregation because we believe they're only able to consume. Adolescence becomes defined as a period of consumption. Teenagers are merely expected to consume education, consume entertainment, and consume products of all sorts.

BEYOND ALIENATED YOUTH

Christian educator David White argues that the dominant culture in America has alienated youth from their proper role as actors and agents in history and offered them carefully circumscribed and woefully benign roles as viewers and consumers.[5] Such a culture domesticates teenagers, alienating them from their own creative agency. Youth ministry has lulled them into consumptive compliance in our churches. Attractional models of youth ministry promote a consumption-driven lifestyle that tempts youth to jettison or ignore the call of God upon their lives to be agents of change in the world. These models relegate youth to "special but marginal status" within the church by giving them their own youth spaces but abstracting them from meaningful participation in the congregation.[6] It presents personal salvation as something to be acquired and tended to on couches in the youth room rather than concerning itself with salvation in all its dimensions. Many churches view adolescents as consumers to be attracted and pleased—a view that stunts the development of youth toward proper human flourishing as agents of the kingdom of God.

Approaching youth ministry from a critical or liberation approach will focus on moving youth toward "embodying the work of Jesus on earth as in heaven," says White.[7] It's not enough to help teenagers reflect on faith and Scripture; this practice must lead beyond reflection to action. Youth ministry must "resist the dominant and domesticating version of adolescence, to invite young people as partners in life and mission," and this is not just a matter of practice, but of true praxis—action that arises from and returns to careful reflection and thought.[8]

BEYOND KNOWLEDGE

A liberation approach to opening the Bible and forming the faith of teenagers challenges two of the assumptions made by other models we've considered.

First, it critiques youth ministry that is more concerned with personal belief or knowledge than action. Too many youth ministries define *discipleship* as a matter of personal belief or individual morality rather than seeing discipleship as a matter of shaping youth into agents of action and transformation in the world. Our common methods of youth ministry are challenged by the critical-liberation idea of Christian formation which leads to action in the world. The earliest theologians of the church would have rejected a ministry to youth that transforms the mind without likewise transforming their actions in the world. Youth ministry that lingers in the youth room must be replaced with learning that invades the world in the form of critically reflective action. It's important that we're clear: Getting students to act is not the goal; bringing students to embody a praxis framework in which their action leads from critical thought and leads back to more critical thought is a key focus. While service projects and mission trips move youth beyond a shallow concern with an inactive personal faith, they usually don't go far enough in helping students awaken to the oppressive realities and structures that are contrary to the Christian message and that need to be challenged. We need to practice youth discipleship that moves beyond a shallow concern with personal salvation reframing the *telos* of youth ministry in terms of human flourishing and the kingdom of God.

Second, it questions the tendency of youth ministry to treat teenagers as objects to be filled with Bible knowledge in order to produce an unquestioned, socialized "faith." Paulo Freire calls this prescriptive-style of education the "banking" concept and adamantly opposes this system as an often unwitting tool of oppression because it presents students with a version of reality for unquestioned acceptance and memorization rather than challenge.

According to Freire, teachers unwittingly domesticate their students in the very process of teaching.[9] The banking model conceives of students as "spectators" of the world who are meant to passively receive into their minds deposits of reality and knowledge as gifts bestowed upon them by teachers who hold knowledge. Rarely is the purpose to think for themselves; even less often is youth ministry a matter of spurring young people to change their world. Youth ministry becomes an unwitting agent of dehumanization if it fails to awaken students to their divine calling as agents of the kingdom of God.

4

A critical pedagogy views participants as actors and creators of change—the vocation of all humans—as opposed to a banking system of education that views students as objects to be filled. Circumscribed roles of student and teacher are replaced in Freire's pedagogy with the notion of student-teachers and teacher-students, each contributing to reflective dialogue that raises consciousness, instead of one contributing the teaching while the other is expected to learn. And these roles unfold, not solely within the neat confines of a classroom, but in the midst of action.

THE SPIRIT OF AWAKENING AND ACTION

Advocates of a liberation approach point to the Spirit as the one who brings inspiration and discernment. It is the Holy Spirit who is teaching us when we gain insight and are awakened through critical reflection as we come to realize there is something wrong with the world. When we begin to question the social mechanisms and cultural construals in new ways, it is the Holy Spirit working in us who fosters our discernment.

Additionally, it isn't in reflection on Scripture that the Spirit's transforming presence is most powerfully encountered, but rather in action. Youth "live in the Spirit of God when they feed the hungry, clothe the naked, visit the imprisoned, shelter the homeless, forgive debts, and offer the poor the Good News: that their misery is not God's intention."[10]

We encounter the work of the Holy Spirit when we resist the spirit of materialism, individualism, oppression, and dehumanization that is pervasive in our culture.

The Holy Spirit is the "source of resistance"[11] who preserves us in such endeavors and, when we engage in making the gospel tangible and discernible in our actions in the world, we become the locus of the Spirit's work.

4

THE ROLE OF TEACHERS

The first task of a teacher in the critical-liberation approach is to foster conscientization, or awakening. This happens through dialogue with others and reflection on the student's personal experiences so that an unmasking of reality occurs and teenagers are able to see reality in a new way. Once teens see reality in a new way, then choosing to act is crucial.

The ultimate goal of this form of pedagogy is humanization which is achieved in the very process of people undertaking thoughtful action to transform the world. There is no room in a liberation approach that consists of mere talk and theory.

Unmasking the oppressive realities and myths of the world is a meaningless exercise unless such unmasking both flows from and toward real action in the world. What's essential, according to theologian and educator Brian Mahan, is that "youth be enabled to recognize, diagnose, and resist the cultural mechanisms that undermine faith, social mechanisms that all too often induce a kind of aesthetic amnesia concerning the great beauty and power of Christian faith."[12]

Teachers and students are equal partners. Teachers seek to empower youth, include them, and encourage them to both see the places in which society contradicts a kingdom ethic and then spur and guide them to activity. Teenagers should be seen as free and responsible and allowed to possess both authority and responsibility for their learning and actions. Too often we separate responsibility and authority when it comes to teenagers. We'll sometimes give them a mandate to accomplish a task, but then assign only low-level responsibilities: Clean your room, pull the weeds, feed the dog. We fear teenagers are not responsible enough to be trusted with tasks that actually matter. This flows from a cultural ideology that views adolescents as incapable.

Closely related to responsibility is authority, and we also fail to give teenagers authority. If responsibility is about getting things done, then authority involves decisions about how things are done. It's about making decisions concerning the nature of the action. Sadly, if teens are only rarely afforded responsibility, it is even more seldom they are given authority. When we give people authority to make decisions but not responsibility to get things done, then we end up with a committee. When people are given responsibility to get things done but have no authority to decide how, we end up with a form of slavery. Empowerment occurs at the precise intersection between the two. When we hold authority and responsibility together, and teenagers are invested with both, then the result is true agency—the ability and call to act and the power to determine how one acts.

In a liberation approach, teachers are those who hold authority and responsibility together for young people as we help them come to consciousness about the oppressive social structures of our world. Then we support and guide them as they exercise authority, decide how to act, and carry out those actions responsibly.

ESSENTIALS FOR TEACHING

Opening the Bible with teenagers should result in them becoming more human—growing and being formed in the ways of the community but also being transformed in ways that push back against the excesses and oppressive aspects of culture. The kingdom of God is antithetical to some of the ways our world is structured politically, economically, and socially:

- poverty
- economic injustice
- violence
- mass incarceration
- racism
- sexism

4

- marginalization of the underemployed
- bullying

We want teenagers to be concerned with the fulfillment of the Great Commandment: to love God and neighbor. This calls for action, but it also calls for rejection of some of the features of American culture. But first teenagers must be awakened from domestication to the values of the surrounding world that stand in contradiction to the gospel. Teenagers are lulled into indifference and complicity to social structures that promote injustice and oppression.

Second, they need to be challenged to action against such structures in light of the in-breaking kingdom of God. What might such actions look like? Consider a church whose plan for youth ministry includes dismantling racism as a result of recognizing the Christian calling to unity and equality.[13] Guided by adults and the praxis loop, teenagers can come up with amazing ideas, such as forming a reconciliation group that meets weekly to pray and discuss together, or forming a multiracial ministry and leadership team that models reconciliation in the youth ministry.

What kind of process might a youth ministry follow to get there? Dan Schipani speaks of three essential movements for educational ministry oriented to justice and liberation as seeing, judging, and acting.[14]

Seeing

The point is to help students discover and understand the conditions and social structures "that generate, sustain, and promote injustice."[15] It is not enough for students to recognize that there is pain, suffering, dehumanization, and injustice in the world. They need help to see these situations from the vantage point of those who suffer and are oppressed and to glimpse the ways in which systemic realities contribute to oppression. Too many mission trips have turned into forms of oppression tourism, permitting Christian teenagers to compassionately gawk at disadvantaged people as if they were animals at a zoo. Such trips usually do little to help teenagers see reality from the vantage of the oppressed or to understand the cultural conditions that allow and promote injustice and oppression.

Judging

What might be God's perspective on the inequality, oppression, and situations faced by people in our world? This step is about comparing and contrasting the difference between the present social situation and the kingdom of God. What is God's design for human flourishing, and how is society structured in such a way to be at odds with this? This step within a liberation approach learning moment is about guiding students to discern how we might act together to announce the in-breaking of God's kingdom in light of cultural reality. How would the world be if the fullness of God's kingdom was already present?[16] In light of God's economy it becomes possible to name injustice and oppression (and the systems and structures that support them) as manifestations of sin. When teenagers come to understand these as expressions of fundamental alienation from God and humanity, they can seek to confront and change them.[17]

Acting

This movement consists of strategizing, planning, and implementing actions that announce the in-breaking kingdom of God by pushing against the systems, structures, and situations of our world that contribute to oppression and dehumanization. Teenagers are moved to seek the transformation of social reality, whether in big or small ways, and in doing so point with their lives and actions to the reign of God that is even now being unveiled.[18]

By setting these three moments of the liberation approach in a loop, it becomes possible to revise the action to which we have committed ourselves in order to determine if it is the most faithful way to move toward social transformation in service to the kingdom of God. It is into this continual praxis loop of reflection and action that our teaching can call young people and thereby move them out of blind acceptance and passive acquiescence to the world they have inherited as young Christians.

METHODS FOR AWAKENING

Youth workers who attempt to employ the liberation approach often struggle with strategies for helping youth interrogate their world and see it with fresh eyes. Numerous methods have been used, but two are worth mentioning here.

First, White points to the power of the "But Why?" method for helping students think about and question any cultural situation or system. The method is simple to employ as it entails repeatedly asking "But why?" to help youth question why social realities and political systems exist the way they do. The game's form mimics the endless "Why?" questions of a young child, but the goal is to expose unquestioned social structures. What cultural beliefs and ideas are hidden behind what we take for granted about the world? Who benefits? Who suffers?

As a practical example of the game in play, consider the statement: "Rosa Parks was arrested." But why was Rosa Parks arrested? The question usually leads the group toward a plain historical answer: "Because she refused to give up her seat on the bus." The facilitator might then ask, "But why was she required to give up her seat?" Because of racist policies in Montgomery that required Black Americans to sit at the back of the bus, might come the answer. "But why were there racist policies?" Continuing this line of questioning leads participants to think through Jim Crow, the vestiges of slavery, and to trace the issue beyond mere acceptance of the way things are. "The conversation might not be linear or include only direct causation, but causes might branch out in many parallel directions that include psychological, ethnic, cultural, economic, political, or religious causes," writes White.[19]

A second method, also described by White, involves a more direct investigation by leading youth through a series of questions around any issue. While full answers to such questions are never possible, asking questions about the situation from various perspectives helps educate and open students' eyes.

- Why does the problematic situation exist?
- How do decisions made by individuals contribute to this problem?
- How do decisions made by the community contribute to this problem?
- How does the history of this community contribute to the problem or issue at hand?
- Which cultural expectations and pressures impact this situation?
- What social institutions reinforce or contribute to this situation?
- How do financial and economic issues play into this situation?
- How do different political views contribute?
- What religious expectations, traditions, or beliefs contribute?
- How do ethnic norms or racial stereotypes contribute to or perpetuate this issue?
- How do human fears and hopes contribute to creating or perpetuating this situation?
- How does a community's concern for present generations, past generations, and future generations play into this issue?

4

CONVERTING THE MIND OF YOUTH

White calls on youth ministry to offer experiences of "intellectual conversion" that awaken youth to the broken complexity of the world and the possibility of becoming agents of healing.[20] Critical thought is "an important dimension of Christian faith," argues White;[21] we love God with our minds when we delight in using our minds to identify the forces that shape our world and then act to transform them.

Practices of discernment and conversation are primary ways to go about revealing and combating cultural distortions. The challenge of Christian teaching is to move young people from naive consciousness to critical consciousness by "using their minds as an act of faith."[22] Naive consciousness lacks an understanding of the social structures and forces that impact our lives, and the result is that we blindly live according to the patterns, systems, and beliefs that have been handed to us by the surrounding culture.[23] Too often youth ministry leaves these unchallenged as the wrong subject matter for education in faith. However, Christian faith stands in opposition to many of these social norms. Therefore, to be formed and truly live as Christian people, it's essential that "youth be enabled to recognize, diagnose, and resist the cultural mechanisms that undermine faith."[24]

By leading youth to use their minds to analyze the complexity of the situations in which they live, they come to see life "constituted by complex relationships with schools, banks, police, families, media, neighborhoods, and prevailing myths, some of which they have the means to change."[25]

White writes about Roberto, a sixteen-year-old African American teen, who attended a summer program committed to engaging youth through critical pedagogy. Roberto and his friends were concerned about the harassment and arrest by police of people of color in their community. White and his colleagues helped Roberto begin to question the reasons for this by engaging in a variety of explorations, interviews, readings, and conversations. In doing so, they helped Roberto and his friends undertake this first step in a liberation approach: seeing the world with fresh eyes. White's role was to facilitate their research by helping them think about how and where to explore for answers.

At the beginning of the process, Roberto and his friends saw the world as a dangerous place in which people of color face oppression without cause and without remedy. However, a new narrative emerged as they explored the situation, one in "which people of color are oppressed, but in which people in partnership with God can also mobilize to change structures."[26]

Roberto and his friends discovered that systemic racism and poverty greatly contributed to the large number of black men in the justice and prison system. But they also discovered that when peers provide positive support, such as through teen courts, many young offenders did not repeat their crimes. White's investigation of these issues with Roberto and his friends resulted in action on their part. Informed with a clearer understanding of the world, they worked to enact their faith by starting teen courts in their high schools.

Obviously, the outcome of this educative process was dramatically different from what happens in most youth ministries and Sunday school classes in churches across the country. And White says that's exactly how it should be. Rather than cultivating people who merely believe a story or adopt a culturally sanctioned religious identity, youth ministry at its best "engages youth as partners in the Kingdom of God, mobilizing the skills, practices, and attitudes to sustain a countercultural Christian faith beyond adolescence into adulthood."[27]

. . . .

Jeremy had more questions about what he'd just read than all three previous approaches combined. While the approach resonated with him on some level, he still didn't quite grasp what it would look like to tackle Sunday school or youth group from a liberation approach perspective. And further, he worried it would make youth ministry too politicized, while possibly not paying enough attention to the spiritual lives of teenagers. He had a lot of thoughts and a lot of questions, but they would have to wait until he could talk to Seymour.

"Oh, yikes, that movie is starting now," Jeremy blurted out as he looked at the time on his phone. Gathering his belongings he rushed out the door of Coffee Haven and into a parking lot that was still under storm deluge. He'd neglected to bring an umbrella and was soaked by the time he reached his car—only to realize he didn't have his keys in his hand. Checking his pockets he finally located the keys but, with his fingers now wet and hopelessly cold, he fumbled them. With a splash the keys disappeared into the murkiness of a parking lot pothole turned puddle. Setting the blue book and his curriculum binder on the top of his car, Jeremy reached into the puddle to find his keys. By this time he was soaked. And, of course, when he tried the key fob, all his furious button-pushing was met with nothing more than a soft squish. He finally unlocked the car door manually and quickly climbed inside. Frustrated and cold, Jeremy revved the engine and sped out of the parking lot, completely oblivious to the flutter of paper and the thud of a blue hardbound book on the pavement behind him.

It wasn't until the next morning when Jeremy pulled into Coffee Haven and saw scads of wet paper plastered to the pavement that he realized what had happened. He wondered why someone would throw litter all over the coffee shop parking lot, then turned in horror to check his backseat for Seymour's book. At that moment he realized those were *his* papers scattered in the lot.

Jeremy was pretty sure Seymour's book was out of print, so replacing it wasn't going to be easy. And besides, he'd lost Seymour's personal copy. The only comfort he took was in knowing that the book had already been missing a few pages when he received it. Nevertheless, he made his way to Oak Harbor Assisted Living to confess his mistake.

"There are worse ways for a book to meet its end," Seymour laughed when Jeremy told him the news.

"What's worse than getting rain soaked, run over, and having your pages torn out?" Jeremy asked, thankful for Seymour's nonchalant response.

"Being left in the library, forgotten, and never read would be far worse," Seymour surmised. "But this one was read, by many people in the past, and most recently by you. So I think it met a happy end. And what did you think of the last chapter I assigned you to read, the one on critical pedagogy and liberation?"

"Honestly, I was royally confused about what this approach would actually look like in the wild. I tried to read that chapter with the prodigal son story in mind, but clearly that Scripture doesn't fit with the liberation approach."

"Aww, not so fast," Seymour countered. "Why do you think it doesn't fit?"

"It's not a story about oppression or dehumanization and has nothing to do with the social structures today's youth face," Jeremy responded. "And besides, Seymour, they've already been through Luke 15 three times in the past few months. I'll get booted out of Oak Harbor if I teach on that passage again."

"Oh, is that true?" Seymour asked with an incredulous tone. "So complaints about the teaching in Sunday school and youth group are increasing?"

"Not exactly," said Jeremy. "If anything the grumbling has declined, but that doesn't mean I'm going to get away with teaching the same Scripture over and over to students week in and week out."

"I'm not surprised that things are going better; you've greatly increased the intentionality with which you open up Scripture with teenagers," Seymour said.

> **Doing anything with intentionality and clear purpose is going to attract energy. But remember, when we have a clear sense of how the Holy Spirit is likely to work in the lives of teenagers, then we're able to do a much better job of positioning them to be formed and transformed by the Spirit.**

"Maybe," Jeremy said, still skeptical as to how much of anything had to do with the Holy Spirit. "But I know this: If you want me to try the liberation teaching approach with students, then we're going to have to find a suitable Scripture."

Seymour quickly said: "You already have one, Jeremy. The prodigal son story has everything you need in order to guide teenagers to see, judge, and act—those three moments of a liberation lesson."

"Well, then help me see how that's possible and act on it, because I'm judging otherwise," Jeremy laughed.

Without missing a beat, Seymour laid it out for him: "Everything in Luke 15 is a response to the Pharisees criticizing Jesus' tendency to welcome and eat with those who were labeled unclean or sinners. The prodigal son story is about Jesus' message that God's response—and our response—shouldn't be to cast people out or hold them at arm's length due to their past or to norms of social exclusion. Instead, the pattern of Christ is to welcome back without penalty those who were lost and now are found. So it seems to me this story has much to say about justice issues and how we deal with social outcasts."

"But Jesus was eating with sinners; he's talking about people who repent of their sins and how those people are welcomed back by God. Of course we should welcome people who are repentant of their sins," Jeremy retorted.

"The category of *sinner* was a broad one in first-century Judaism, Jeremy. Physical infirmity was often considered a sign of sin, so if you were blind or crippled, you were likely to be placed in the sinner category. The same with those who didn't follow dietary law or ritual cleansing. Those with leprosy? Sinners. I think there's plenty of room to understand this story as primarily Jesus' way of talking about how his followers should respond to those who want to be restored after having been outcast by society, whether by their own choices or as a result of life's circumstances."

Jeremy pondered this perspective for a moment before Seymour continued: "So, to teach from a liberation approach with this Scripture, I think you simply help students see (and name) more clearly those who are considered outcast and why. Then, guide them to use the Scripture to judge how followers of Christ should be responding to those who are outcast in ways that are different from how society has responded. Finally, I think you help students make choices about how they're going to spring into action to help restore those who are outcast."

"Restore them spiritually?" Jeremy asked.

"I meant restore them to standing and life within the community, but yes, you could think about it spiritually as well. The two may not be as disconnected as we often think," Seymour responded.

Jeremy sighed, "This feels overwhelming at some level. How am I supposed to do this in an hour?"

Seymour laughed uncontrollably. Then he continued laughing to the point that Jeremy laughed along, though he didn't understand what was so funny. "An hour?" Seymour finally squeaked out as he regained his composure. "Son, you can't accomplish all this in an hour. You need to start thinking outside of the box a little bit. Yes, you have an hour for Sunday school and an hour for youth group, but why do you have to think about limiting your teaching and formation of youth to those times?"

"Because if class goes long …" Jeremy started.

"No! That's not what I meant!" Seymour roared, simultaneously laughing and showing frustration that Jeremy wasn't understanding. "Look, rather than trying to confine your liberation approach to an hour in a classroom, here's what I want you to do: Don't write a thing."

"Nothing?"

"Nada, zilch," Seymour replied. "I simply want you to show up to class this week. Use a blank chalkboard or markerboard, or whatever kind of board you have these days, and then read the story to your group. After reading the story, ask, 'Who are the people in our society who are considered sinners and outcasts because of their individual choices (like the prodigal son) or because of life circumstances outside their control?' Then, I want you to list on the markerboard the different categories of people they call out."

"That will take like two minutes," Jeremy scoffed.

"Good, because that leaves you 58 minutes to discuss together why those people are outcasts, what they have done to make themselves outcasts, and what society has done to make them outcasts," Seymour said. "And you're going to map all of that out on the board. And then you're going to let them choose one category of persons, and you're going to assemble some volunteers to go out over the next week and find someone who fits that description, and then you're going to do something radical ... "

"Radical? Like what?" Jeremy asked puzzled.

"Yes, something very radical. Are you ready for this?" Seymour whispered, leaning in. "You're going to *talk* to this person."

"About *what*?" Jeremy whispered, unaware that he was matching Seymour's hushed tones.

Seymour explained: "You're going to ask about the person's life, experiences, and find out who this person is. You're going to get to know this person with your students. And the goal is for them to see this person in all of her or his humanity and to come to a greater understanding of all the complex reasons why this person continues to live as an outcast from mainstream society."

"And then what?" Jeremy asked.

"Well, then you're going to have this team of students come back and report to the rest of the group about the person they met, describing what they learned about why this person is in the situation he or she is in," Seymour outlined. "Then you're going to lead them in a discussion that *judges* what the response of Christian people should be based on the response of the father in the prodigal son story. And when they've determined that the church should be responding—and they *will* make that determination—you're going to guide them into thinking about how they can *act* for this particular person, or for that whole category of people, in ways that are commensurate with the restorative embrace of the father."

Jeremy sat stunned for a long time, staring into space. Seymour made it sound so simple, but he was fearful his students wouldn't respond, and in truth—he was more fearful they would. After an awkwardly long pause, Jeremy finally confessed: "All this makes me nervous because, to be honest, I don't actually want to leave the youth room. I like it when teaching the Bible lesson takes exactly an hour. I like teaching in my little box of a classroom, and I like my box of an hour-long time frame because ... well ... because it's safe and it doesn't require very much of me. But this. This requires ... ," Jeremy trailed off.

"Action," Seymour said, completing his sentence. "And faith. It requires not only believing that the Holy Spirit, The Teacher, is ready to breathe into the lives of your students but also a willingness for that same Spirit to transform your students and you—and the world in the process. You know, Jeremy, maybe one of the reasons we talk so little about the work of the Holy Spirit in youth ministry is that deep down we think it's better not to have any idea of how we're going to bring our students into the spaces where and the times when the Holy routinely shows up. Because when the Holy Spirit *does* show up, fire falls from heaven and consumes everything we've placed upon the altar, 'even the water in the trough around it.' So I wonder if sometimes we're actually trying to avoid the Holy Spirit who is in the habit of disrupting, upending, and turning our little boxes inside out."

. . . .

When Sunday arrived, Jeremy read aloud the now familiar prodigal son story, then wrote Seymour's question on the markerboard:

Who in our world are considered sinners and outcasts—whether as a result of their individual choices or by circumstances outside of their control?

Students began calling out responses, and Jeremy listed the categories on the board just as they described them: Immigrants, drug users, alcoholics, homosexuals, the homeless, criminals, fat people, ugly people, persons with disabilities, persons with autism, and Jeremy's favorite category—because it so typified life in Oak Harbor—people who don't like football.

Then Jeremy began to help his teenagers think through and map out all the various reasons that people in each category experienced both hardship and societal rejection.

"Drug addicts are addicts because they made a stupid choice to use drugs, and they got hooked," said a student named Brooke.

"They might have chosen to do drugs, but I doubt if they knew they would get addicted," countered a pock-faced boy named Mitch.

"Sometimes people turn to drugs because their lives are pretty hopeless," Jenny chimed in. "My aunt almost died of drugs, but she started to use them because her husband and my sweet little niece died in a car wreck. She was so sad. I think at first the drugs made her feel better." There was silence in the room for a moment while the group soberly considered the personal depth of what Jenny had shared.

Finally Cameron, an older teen sitting in the corner, asked, "Can I add some reasons to the homeless category?"

"Sure," Jeremy said.

"I'm sure you all know David, the homeless guy who stands on the corner down by the Kroger. Well, I've talked to him before ..."

"What?! You've talked to him?" interrupted a tall boy named Terrence.

"I know who you're talking about, but I didn't know he had a name," Brooke added.

"Yeah, I talked to him once and, yes, he has a name. It's David. And he told me he's homeless because, even though he actually has a job of sorts, he doesn't make enough money to pay for food, gas, *and* pay rent. So he lives in his car because it's all he can afford if he, you know, still wants to eat and stuff."

"Why does he even have a car? He's homeless," Terrence queried. Then he continued, "And I'm sure he doesn't have enough money to pay rent because he's buying booze to drink."

Jeremy jumped in to guide and temper the discussion, but it continued to pique the students' interest long enough for them to realize there are a host of reasons why someone might be homeless.

As a result of the discussion, Jeremy invited several students, including Cameron, Terrence, and Brooke, to join him in a visit with David later that week. A few days later, together with Jeremy, those students approached David on the street corner one afternoon following school. He was leery of their intentions at first, but soon warmed to them. They ended up spending nearly two hours with him at McDonald's, talking about his life, his past, and the circumstances surrounding his homelessness in Oak Harbor.

As it turned out, David was originally from Connecticut but had bounced around Tennessee for several years. He had ended up in Oak Harbor when his car broke down the previous year as he was headed to the city to find work. He'd used the last of his money to fix his car and, at that point, decided to stay put. He had applied for disability a few years prior, but the money had never come through. Nevertheless, he found it difficult to work because of previous injuries he'd sustained. Potential employers considered him damaged goods. David was smart and articulate, and the students were surprised. They had expected someone crazy and strung out on drugs or alcohol. David did admit that he spent a lot of time drinking, and it was clear that he likely had some kind of substance abuse problem.

Overall the meeting was eye-opening and, during the next Sunday school class, the students who met David spent considerable time sharing everything they learned about him. "So, in a lot of ways," Brooke said as she wrapped up the group's report on David, "he's like the prodigal son: He's hungry, out of money, and he wants a job. Oh, and I guess he spends his money in some of the same bad ways as the prodigal son because he drinks a lot, too."

Sensing a shift in the conversation, Jeremy decided they were finally ready to move to the second step of judging. He framed the transition to the second step with a question:

Based upon what we learn about God's grace and love for the lost in the prodigal son story, in what ways should our response to David and homelessness differ from the response of the surrounding culture?

The discussion was rich. The students concluded that the community considered David as a nuisance, someone less than human whom they should avoid and as someone who was paying for his personal mistakes. Yet, they knew that David's situation was complex and that a lot of different factors had contributed to his situation of being homeless. "And even if it were all his fault," Brooke explained, "the prodigal son story reminds us that the father would still welcome him back and help him, just a we should, because he's a child of God."

"So what should we do?" Jeremy asked. "What actions do you think we should take on behalf of David and other folks who are homeless in our area?" The students brainstormed ideas for a while. Amidst typical suggestions of buying him meals and providing him a space to sleep, there were also creative responses born out of understanding the complex dynamics of the situation.

"What would help him most is having a job," Cameron said.

"And somebody needs to help him figure out his disability, or government assistance, or whatever he's supposed to be receiving," Terrence chimed in.

"And honestly, I think he needs somebody to talk to regularly, not just one time," remarked Brooke.

By the end of the hour, they had devised a plan:

- Several students were assigned to research business owners in the congregation who might be able to offer David a job.

- With the help of Jeremy, Terrence was going to approach a lawyer in the congregation who they thought might be able to help with the disability claims.

- Brooke was going to schedule several opportunities over the next few months for students to get together with David for lunch.

As Jeremy turned off the lights in the Sunday school room, he was overwhelmed with all that had transpired. Just a few weeks prior, he had dreaded the thought of teaching here, but now with intentionality and clarity of goals, he was seeing vibrancy in the youth ministry. *And in Sunday school no less*, he thought. *Miraculous*!

Download the full leader's guide for Jeremy's liberation approach lesson on the prodigal son by visiting *http://www. youthministrypartners.com/tob.*

Endnotes

[1] Discussed in *Youth, Gospel, Liberation, Third Edition*, by Michael Warren (ACTA Publications, 2000); page 10.

[2] Discussed in *Youth, Gospel, Liberation*; page 27.

[3] Discussed in *Consuming Youth: Leading Teens Through Consumer Culture*, by John Berard, Rick Bartlett, and James Penner (Zondervan/Youth Specialties; 2010).

[4] The components of this adolescent script are unpacked in *Consuming Youth*.

[5] Discussed in *Awakening Youth Discipleship: Christian Resistance in a Consumer Culture*, by Brian J. Mahan, Michael Warren, and David White (Wipf and Stock Publishing, 2008); page 19.

[6] From *Awakening Youth Discipleship*; page 19.

[7] From *Awakening Youth Discipleship*; page 19.

[8] From *Awakening Youth Discipleship*; page 19.

[9] Discussed in *Pedagogy of the Oppressed*, by Paulo Freire (Bloomsbury Academic, 2000); page 56.

[10] From *Awakening Youth Discipleship*; 52-53.

[11] From *Awakening Youth Discipleship*; page 88.

[12] From *Awakening Youth Discipleship*; pages 89-90.

[13] Discussed in *Mapping Christian Education: Approaches to Congregational Learning*, by Jack L. Seymour (Abingdon Press, 1997); page 25.

[14] Discussed in *Mapping*; page 33.

[15] From *Mapping*; page 33.

[16] Discussed in *Mapping*; page 33.

[17] Discussed in *Mapping*; page 33.

[18] Discussed in *Mapping*; page 34.

[19] From *Awakening Youth Discipleship*; page 32; White actually begins his example of the game with the statement, "Rosa Parks' feet hurt," but this can too easily lead to the mistaken idea that Parks refused to give up her seat at the front of the bus because her feet hurt, a notion that she disputed.

[20] From *Awakening Youth Discipleship*; page 23.

[21] From *Awakening Youth Discipleship*; page 24.

[22] From *Awakening Youth Discipleship*; page 23.

[23] Discussed in *Awakening Youth Discipleship*; page 26.

[24] From *Awakening Youth Discipleship*; page 89.

[25] From *Awakening Youth Discipleship*; page 26.

[26] From *Awakening Youth Discipleship*; page 27.

[27] From *Awakening Youth Discipleship*; page 37.

CHAPTER 5: REVISITING THE CONTEMPLATIVE APPROACH

It was a brisk morning when Jeremy next found his way to Oak Harbor Assisted Living, room 231. The door was ajar when he arrived, and so he poked his head in without knocking, calling Seymour's name as he did. He was greeted by silence, and so he called again as he entered the quiet apartment. Noticing a handwritten note and some paper on Seymour's chair, he took a look and was pleasantly surprised to find it was for him.

"Gone for a jog—or what you might call a walk. Read the attached article before I get back," the note stated in jittery, cursive handwriting. And there was a P.S. at the bottom: "And make some fresh coffee. I like it strong."

With the blue book destroyed, Jeremy thought he'd escaped from anymore of Seymour's reading assignments. He'd underestimated the old man's fortitude, however, and his access to a printer. The article attached to the note was printed from the Internet and stapled nicely in the upper-left corner; the title across the top read, "Revisiting the Contemplative Approach."

Jeremy went into the kitchen and rinsed out the coffee pot. Now, finally, here was an approach that felt familiar. He'd experienced some contemplative youth ministry during his first few church visits as a middle school student. As he scooped coffee grounds into the filter and filled the carafe, he thought to himself, *Funny, how fitting this is, considering that I'm about to invest some time in the contemplative approach.* He remembered the two most important things during his first days in youth group as a middle schooler: coffee and walking a prayer labyrinth. He didn't like coffee at the time and had found the prayer labyrinth to be weird, since no one had ever explained to him the meaning of walking a maze for Jesus.

The coffee finished brewing, so Jeremy poured himself a cup and sat down to read the article Seymour had left for him …

During the 2000's, youth ministry became increasingly enamored with contemplative practices. Many ministries traded disco balls, comfy couches, and messy games for candles, centering prayer, and *lectio divina*. But soon into this supposed renaissance in spiritual practices, the glow faded and many youth ministers dusted off the mothballed games-and-glam approach and packed away the coffee, candles, and contemplation that typified their appropriation of the contemplative.

What happened? Was the contemplative approach to opening the Bible with teenagers found wanting? In actuality, I'd suggest that despite dripping a lot of candle wax on the youth room carpet, many ministries that "went contemplative" never fully understood nor embraced the approach. Myths about what the approach entailed abounded: It's about using candles. It requires silence. It's very individualistic. It doesn't pay attention to the Bible. It's rooted in new age thought. The idea that a contemplative approach was primarily an aesthetic change, along with the various myths that persisted, together overshadowed the true heart of the approach in many locales. It's worth looking deeper at aspects of a contemplative approach to youth ministry and how such an approach would undergird and change our approaches to opening the Bible with youth.

The aim of contemplative youth ministry is to "be attentive to God's presence, discerning of the Spirit," as a community that accompanies "young people on the way of Jesus."[1] No candles required. The central problem in sharing the Christian faith with young people doesn't concern words; it's deeper than that. Contemplative proponent Mark Yaconelli writes: "The real crisis facing those of us who seek to share faith with youth is this: We don't know how to be with our kids. We don't know how to be with ourselves. We don't know how to be with God."[2]

The contemplative approach is a call to "Slow down and receive the young people in our lives."[3] Yaconelli writes that contemplation in youth ministry is about modeling for young people an openness of heart that affords us receptivity to the Holy Spirit and an attentiveness to God that forms young people in the compassion of Jesus.[4]

In contrast to the fast pace of contemporary life, contemplation calls teenagers to be present in the moment and to be aware of God's presence with them.

The contemplative approach borrows generously from Christian monastics and mystics. Rather than placing emphasis on the actions of the teacher skilled in educational method, the contemplative approach casts the youth leader as the abbot charged with fostering an environment for listening to God. In monastic tradition, the role of the abbot is not primarily to impart knowledge, but to structure the life of the community for times of listening to God and one another in various forms of contemplative prayer, worship, dialogue, and action. Compare this to many forms of youth ministry in which the youth minister is perceived to function as the captain, the chief cook, or the cruise ship recreation director. In other words, among other things, we continually instruct or engage teens without attempting to allow God to engage them.

5

Contemplation in a Christian framework has always focused heavily on prayer and attentiveness to God through rumination on Scripture. In this way a contemplative approach to opening Scripture is not new, though after several centuries of emphasis in the West on dissecting Scripture verse by verse, parsing words, digging for the original meaning, and seeking the objective meaning of the text, the contemplative approach might seem new with its focus on the spiritual reading of Scripture.

Those who take a contemplative approach believe that the Holy Spirit not only inspired the Bible but also still speaks to individual human hearts in unique ways when Scripture is read and considered. Opening Scripture becomes a conduit or means through which teenagers become attentive to, and discerning of, the voice of God.

The contemplative approach puts the focus on the work of the Holy Spirit as the Teacher who speaks, guides, and forms us while we abide in God's presence.

The role of the youth worker is to alleviate distractions and anxiety in order to allow the community to rest in God, listen to God, and follow God together. Inviting youth to become attentive and to interact directly with the text in ways that make them attentive to God are important to contemplative practitioners.

Despite the fact that Christianity is based upon the presence and activity of God in our world—that is what we mean when we refer to the Incarnation, the God who moved into the neighborhood— we have nevertheless often in the history of Christianity banished ideas of direct experience and encounter with God. We have preferred to focus instead on telling people about God, attempting to give them knowledge about God, rather than leading them to an experience of God. However, increasingly in a secularized and pluralistic culture where it is difficult to believe in God, it is the experience of God that makes faith possible. The Roman Catholic theologian Karl Rahner said about this, "The devout Christian of the future will either be a mystic, one who has experienced something, or he will cease to be anything at all."[5]

In this approach, creating space for God becomes a main task of youth ministry. Ensuring that there are times of gathering as Christians for prayer and discernment away from the distraction of the world, but always sent back to the world, is central. Thus, while some other approaches are primarily concerned with applying biblical truth to young lives, or helping youth interpret their lives in light of the gospel story, the contemplative approach is concerned with helping youth be attentive to God. "We move away from anxious concern with creating entertaining programming or doctrinally sound instruction and toward a peaceful and prayerful attention to God's presence in the lives of young persons,"[6] writes an advocate of the contemplative approach. The contemplative approach is not just pointing out to youth that God will show up in their lives, but rather it involves giving them space and leading them in that space to allow God to speak and to guide them.

COMMUNAL AND ACTION-ORIENTED

Opening the Bible with youth using a contemplative framework shouldn't result in an overly individualistic focus. Rather, the community shares together what each is hearing from God and discerns together as a community how the community should respond. The structure of youth meetings, whether Sunday school or youth group, then becomes set by a "liturgy of discernment" designed to lead the group together toward shared space for discerning God's voice and call. It is likely that such a liturgy will include times of silence, rest, meditation on Scripture, reflection, and discussion of what God is showing, revealing, and doing. The liturgy often employs a host of historical spiritual practices from a variety of Christian traditions such as Ignatian awareness examen, *lectio divina*, centering prayer, The Jesus Prayer, and simple silence.

5

Additionally, the end result of a contemplative approach should not be navel gazing but a communal sense of calling by God to be sent back into the world with new action, not just new knowledge.

Far from banishing fun and craziness from youth ministry, Mark Yaconelli advocates for including whatever effectively allows youth to discern the call of God. He writes specifically about one youth group that needed regular times of bowling together in order to reduce anxiety and distractions and allow them to focus on God in their times of group discernment.[7]

The point is that the youth minister as abbot doesn't include such times merely as a way to attract youth; rather they're included in order to properly structure the sabbath rhythm of work, play, and rest and allow young people to be present and attentive to God. This means that teachers who desire to utilize this approach need to be attentive to the entire ecology of the teaching/learning event, rather than just the formal educational time. For example, all aspects of a Wednesday night youth group meeting (games, snacks, friendly conversation, and so on) need to be appropriately structured to support and lead toward the opportunity for youth to be ready to discern the voice of God.

Those who take a contemplative approach to communicating the gospel realize that for young people, it will be through being led to an experience of God that they will be enabled to truly embrace the gospel.

> **And what is this gospel? It is that God loves us deeply and unconditionally and that Christ died for us, even when we were of no discernible value.**

The contemplative approach brings us not merely to hear the gospel but to experience it. It is in discerning the voice and presence of God that we experience our "own deepest identity as beloved."[8]

The most difficult thing for teachers who utilize a contemplative approach is the loss of control, or at least the loss of a sense of control, they have in directing the formational process. We like to make ourselves feel good by pointing to exactly what we taught and what was learned in any teaching moment. But that desire arises from our anxiety, and the "big ideas" we want to point to don't actually measure anything except our anxiety. The contemplative approach has to be rooted in letting go of anxiety and believing that God will work and speak.

In order to do this, teachers must themselves believe and experience the truth that they are in fact the beloved of God. The spiritual life of the teacher is certainly important in the contemplative approach, and teachers cannot neglect themselves and focus upon merely awakening youth to the love of God. In fact, a contemplative approach demands quite the opposite. Theologian and contemplative advocate Michael Hryniuk writes, "If we adults who minister with youth do not respond to our own longing to know and love God, we will have nothing of value to offer young persons in their quest."[9] In this approach, the ability to communicate the good news of God's unconditional and all-encompassing love requires adult guides who believe and experience this themselves.

GUIDING YOUTH CONTEMPLATIVELY

South African youth worker and author Mark Tittley defines four roles for the teacher in a contemplative approach that are distinct from those usually conceived for teachers.[10] Where an instructional approach conceives of teachers as those who are able to notice and point out important truths embedded in Scripture, a contemplative approach places emphasis on the teacher's (or guide's) ability to notice and point out signs of God in the lives of students. Consequently, a contemplative approach sees teachers more as spiritual directors than scriptural exegetes. The four main aspects to the role of spiritual director are the following:

5

Preparing

It is the teacher's role to encourage students to look, listen, and become aware of God in all aspects of their experience, not just in the designated receiving times of the contemplative lesson. Prodding and preparing youth to experience God in common places is crucial. Asking questions such as, "How is God present?" or "Where have you noticed signs of God?" prepare students to be attuned to the divine presence. Tittley points out that Jesus promised to be present where two or three are gathered and that people in the New Testament encountered Jesus while they were engaged in everyday practices of life, including eating, working, and traveling. Likewise, teenagers should be prepared to experience God in their everyday lives, not just in the silence of Scripture reading.

Pointing

Spiritual directors in a contemplative approach don't just prepare teenagers to experience God; they also should actively notice and point to the presence of God in the lives of youth, thereby helping teens come to their own recognition. Watching carefully for when teenagers evidence the fruit of the Spirit or act in ways commensurate with the grace of Christ can be opportunities to point to God's activity in the life of a student.

Naming

It's important to help teenagers mark and name their experiences of God's presence by helping them find theological language that describes their experiences. This is a matter of listening to youth and finding places of connection between their stories and the wealth of theological description embedded in Christian tradition. This should not be confused with choosing a doctrine to teach; the discussion of theology and doctrine should arise organically out of the discussion of the student's experience. Inviting teenagers

5

into testimony and journaling are two ways to help them begin the process of exploring and naming their experiences.

Nurturing

We nurture the ability of teenagers to discern the voice and activity of God by providing opportunities for creative prayer and listening experiences. Leading students into contemplative practice in our formal teaching times nurtures their ability to listen for God in Scripture both individually and corporately.

COMPONENTS OF CONTEMPLATIVE TEACHING

Tittley suggests six moments of a contemplative approach lesson that should anchor a time of teaching and nurture in this approach.[11]

Ritual

First, an opening ritual should mark the beginning of a sacred time and space and draw the group's attention to the presence of God. Tittley recommends that the ritual be rather short (less than two minutes) and should draw the entire group into participation rather than relying on just one person to perform the ritual. This could be a corporate song, lighting of candles, or a responsive reading. Whatever marks well the separation of the time from the ordinary and reminds participants that attentiveness to the presence of God is the purpose of gathering.

Relating

Recognition of one another's presence must go hand in hand with recognizing God's presence. The work that is done in the contemplative approach is not intended to be solitary but communal, and attending to one another in deep listening will prepare the group to operate together rather than separately.

5

Receiving

After welcoming God and one another, taking time to become fully attentive to God's presence and to discern the Spirit's voice becomes of paramount importance. The teacher might lead the group in various prayer practices that allow students to become attentive to God and to Scripture. *Lectio divina* and the Ignatian Awareness Examen are among common prayer practices for this time, though any activity that draws students to listen for God can be used.

Lectio divina (literally, divine reading), an ancient method by which listeners are given the opportunity to "chew" on the Word, is among the most popular methods for opening Scripture. A short passage of Scripture is selected and is read several times slowly by a reader. Those gathered listen to the Scripture reading and allow a word or phrase to catch their attention or interest. Then, in a period of silence, listeners are asked to simply pray that God will reveal the specific meaning or implication for their lives and why this word or phrase might be a conduit for God speaking to them through Scripture.

Many practices suitable for this moment bring students to ruminate on the Scripture or listen for a word or phrase that stands out to them before they wait and listen for insight from God.

Reflecting

In this time students share what they have noticed, heard, or realized from God through the Scripture. As each person is given an opportunity to speak, the others should be listening for threads of commonality to discern how God is speaking to the group as a whole.

Responding

Together the group should move beyond considering what God might be saying to the group in order to focus on how God might be calling the group to act. Questions such as the following might be helpful:

- In light of all that we've heard and shared, what is God saying to us about what we need to be doing as a group?

The focus of the reflection time is to determine a trajectory for the group to move from listening to action. This does not necessarily have to result in a single, unified idea for action, but it may be that various subsets of the group feel that God is calling them to respond in diverse ways.

Returning

As the session comes to an end, it is appropriate to offer a closing prayer or benediction that sends members of the group back into ordinary time to act upon what they have recognized and heard from God.

. . . .

Finishing the article, Jeremy put it aside and finished off the last swig of coffee in his cup. Now that he understood the meaning and intention behind the contemplative approach, he had a very different view of what the approach could be and how it differed from his previous personal experience. It was clear that his youth leader in middle school had used some of the contemplative methods, but without fully understanding what he was doing or why. "I did a lot of sleeping while we were supposedly meditating," Jeremy said aloud and laughed, remembering how he'd once curled up in a ball and slept for over an hour while the leaders assumed he was praying and having a spiritual moment. *I think all I discerned was that the carpet in the church basement smelled musty*, Jeremy thought.

The experiences he had with contemplative methods as a teenager always felt isolating. Even though he would do the activities, like the prayer labyrinth or a prayer station, he was always alone. There wasn't much of a community component, and the lack of a relational component was part of the reason he had resented the experience. Additionally, Jeremy never remembered anything meaningful coming out of the contemplative meetings he'd attended. People didn't talk about what they'd heard or experienced, and they certainly didn't talk about actions the group thought God was leading them to take collectively.

As Jeremy thought about what it would look like to use a contemplative teaching approach in his church, he thought about occasionally reformatting Sunday school to include a contemplative lesson. *What if I did a monthly rotation and we took a contemplative approach one week, and then maybe an interpretive approach another, and so on?* Jeremy thought.

Seymour came bungling through the door, clumsily dropping his keys. Startled by Jeremy's presence, he dropped his mail on the floor, too, then said: "Oh, Jeremy, I'd almost forgotten you were coming. I left you something to read."

"Found it. Read it," said Jeremy, chuckling to himself at Seymour's fluster.

"And did you discover what the contemplative approach is all about?" Seymour questioned.

"Well, I sort of came into it thinking it was just about turning the lights down low and rearranging the furniture, but I realize now it's about practicing the presence of God and helping teenagers develop habits and practices to discern the voice and presence of God."

As the words came out of Jeremy's mouth, he immediately realized a problem with his plan for rotational Sunday school and said: "Wait a second, the contemplative approach falls apart if it's just something we tack onto our teaching every now and then."

The point isn't simply to expose teenagers to contemplative methods but to help students develop an ongoing practice of discerning and listening for the voice of God.

Jeremy continued: "If I as a teacher am not always operating like a spiritual director helping youth by preparing, pointing, naming, and nurturing, then I'm going to fall into the trap of saying my ministry includes contemplative components but with very little benefit."

"True, true," said Seymour, as Jeremy realized he'd been talking out loud for the last few seconds. "The fullness of the contemplative approach in the life of a teenager happens when we help them to become continually aware of God's voice and presence, rather than just leading them to pay attention to the spiritual sense of Scripture here and there."

"You know, we have the fall retreat coming up," Jeremy said. "What if we turned the entire retreat into a time for contemplation and awareness of God's presence. We can invite students to come and slow down for the weekend, and we can create an environment where they become attuned to God's voice and presence. We can use the retreat opportunity to help students begin developing some ongoing prayer practices in their lives. And we can also use it to train our adult volunteers to think of their roles more as spiritual guides than chaperones. I'm thinking that a lot of people may have believed the power of the contemplative approach is in the prayer and Scripture exercises that the teenagers engage. But perhaps the broader power is in reframing the task of the teacher as a spiritual guide who walks with teenagers and is continually involved in practices that help teenagers build awareness of God."

"I think you may be on to something," Seymour said. "And, while you're at it, I know the perfect Scripture passage to explore as your retreat theme."

"Let me guess: Luke 15, the prodigal son?" Jeremy said rolling his eyes. Seymour just smiled.

．．．．

The leaves had turned colors and most had fallen from the trees by the time the Oak Harbor church bus pulled up to the lodge at Mt. Carmel Retreat Center in the foothills of the Smokey Mountains. Contrary to his usual approach of promising unending fun and craziness, Jeremy had advertised the fall retreat as a time to rest and contemplate. "Slow down, be with friends, take a walk, learn to pray, sleep in, and listen for the voice of God—maybe for the first time ever," read his social media posts for the retreat. With an advertisement like that he had wondered if anyone would sign up to attend. He was astounded when the number of registrants exceeded the previous year.

Jeremy hadn't booked a worship band nor was there a funny and entertaining guest speaker. And most everything he'd planned was designed to do exactly what he'd promised: slow down the teenagers. He'd taken seriously the idea that the teacher should be like an abbot, structuring the community's ability to be attentive to God, so he'd planned every activity with that in mind. A leisurely morning schedule allowed—actually demanded—that students sleep in. "Nobody out of bed before 6:45 a.m." was literally the first rule of retreat. And if students wanted to be up that early, their only option was "morning prayer" with one of the adult volunteers.

Jeremy had scheduled a chapel service after a late breakfast, but this time was to be used for teaching students various prayer and journaling techniques and was centered on *lectio divina*. Following the *lectio* portion of chapel, students gathered with their cabin groups to discuss what they'd heard and experienced through the Scripture. These groups were led by volunteers whom Jeremy had trained as spiritual guides and who understood the meaning of preparing, pointing, naming, and nurturing, the four functions Jeremy had learned from the article Seymour had provided. In addition to discussing what they experienced individually, the cabin guides were ready to discern with students what God might be saying to the group collectively and how God might be leading them to respond and act.

Afternoon free-time options were arranged to encourage rest and relationships. For the evening, Jeremy had planned various group experiences that ultimately led students back to their cabin groups for more discussion and reflection on what they'd experienced. The entire retreat was decidedly different from anything he'd done before, but he shocked even himself when he decided that the first evening experience would be an invitation for students to walk a labyrinth.

"Really?" Seymour had asked when informed of the plan. "You told me the one thing you hated in middle school was walking the labyrinth."

"But now I think that's because none of us truly understood why we were walking it, and there was never much debriefing time. But if we correct those things, then a labyrinth is perfect for the story of the prodigal son because it reminds us of the journey of faith—sometimes when we're feeling a million miles from God, we're actually just around the corner. Along the way in the labyrinth there will be stopping points and, at each one, students will prayerfully reflect and journal on a question, such as:

- God, in what areas of my life am I close to you right now?
- Jesus, in what areas of my life am I far from you?
- Father, in what parts of my life am I actively running away from you to do as I please?

- Holy Spirit, in what areas of my life do I need to recognize the foolishness of going my own way?
- God, in each of these, how can I begin the journey home?

"Those are profound questions, Jeremy. I think that could be a very powerful time," Seymour said.

Jeremy continued: "Also, we're not going to just leave students with their individual thoughts and prayers. When they exit the labyrinth, they'll quietly join their cabin groups and their cabin guides will lead them through sharing collectively all they experienced as well as how they plan to respond not only as they return home but also in the days ahead. We want them not only to take the bus home from retreat but also to begin a spiritual journey home toward God."

Seymour didn't say a word; he simply nodded and beamed with pride and contentment. Over the past several months he'd watched Jeremy make his own journey—a journey of discovery in teaching and forming young people in the faith. Not only had Jeremy learned to teach outside the box using different approaches, but also he'd gained the ability to conceive of the Holy Spirit's work in the lives of teenagers in diverse ways.

At first Jeremy could see nothing but his personal futile and flailing efforts to teach youth. Now he could see a world teeming with opportunities for the Holy Spirit to ignite the faith of youth. This was a world ready for teachers to position and prepare teenagers to encounter the life-transforming, awe-inspiring Spirit of God. Seymour saw all of these changes, but he said nothing. Instead, he recalled the words of Elijah in 1 Kings 17:37-39 who positioned the altar and prayed for The Teacher to teach:

> Answer me, LORD! Answer me so that this people will know that you, LORD, are the real God and that you can change

their hearts." Then the LORD's fire fell; it consumed the sacrifice, the wood, the stones, and the dust. It even licked up the water in the trench! All the people saw this and fell on their faces.

"Amen," said Seymour softly.

Download the full leader's guide for Jeremy's contemplative approach lesson on the prodigal son by visiting *http://www. youthministrypartners.com/tob.*

Endnotes

[1] From "The Journey of the Beloved: A Theology of Youth Ministry" by Michael Hryniuk, in *Growing Souls: Experiments in Contemplative Youth Ministry*, edited by Mark Yaconelli (Zondervan/Youth Specialties); page 62.

[2] From *Contemplative Youth Ministry: Practicing the Presence of Jesus*, by Mark Yaconelli (Zondervan/Youth Specialties, 2006); page 19.

[3] From *Contemplative Youth Ministry*; page 24.

[4] From *Contemplative Youth Ministry*; page 25.

[5] From *The Practice of Faith*, by Karl Rahner (The Crossroads Publishing Company, 1986); pages 69-77.

[6] From "Journey of the Beloved," *Growing Souls*; page 78.

[7] Discussed in *Contemplative Youth Ministry*; pages 227-228.

[8] From *Growing Souls*; page 67.

[9] From *Growing Souls*; page 67.

[10] Discussed in "Contemplative Youth Ministry" by Mark Tittley at *www.ymresourcer.com/documents/Contemplative_Youth_Ministry.doc*.

[11] Discussed in "Contemplative Youth Ministry" at *ymresourcer.com*.

APPENDIX: LEADING YOUTH IN THEOLOGICAL REFLECTION

Jeremy and the Oak Harbor youth were on a mission trip in Nashville when Ricardo told a story during the evening debriefing: "My group went to get coffee this afternoon, and the craziest thing happened. It made us angry in a lot of ways. While we waited, we started talking to a homeless man sitting on the patio, and we offered to buy him a drink. When we went inside to order for him, the barista told us that we weren't allowed to buy him a drink. She literally would not let us buy a drink because it was for a homeless guy." The room buzzed with reactions.

Meanwhile Jeremy wondered which adult volunteer had taken a group for coffee when they were supposed to be working. Shaking off the thought, he tried to formulate a response. "Well," Jeremy gulped. "It's shocking how people are sometimes treated, but that's why we're on this trip: to shine Christ's light, and, um, to bring hope to people who often are discarded by the world."

The group remained silent. He knew they were waiting for him to say more—something less canned and cliché. Instead he asked sheepishly, "Anybody else have a high or a low to share?"

Later that evening, Jeremy tiptoed out of the guys' bunk room and sent an e-mail from his phone: *Seymour, I hope you're checking e-mail these days. I need some advice. Tonight on the mission trip I asked teens to share highs and lows from the day. One student told about his work team's encounter with a homeless man. When they tried to purchase a drink for him, they were denied service. The students were shocked. We all were shocked, but I had no idea how to respond. All I could muster were some platitudes. Got any wisdom for me? All the best from Nashville, Jeremy.*

The next day Jeremy was pleased to find a response from Seymour with a link to an article. "Read this, it might help," Seymour wrote tersely. Jeremy clicked the link and began to read . . .

. . . .

THE ART OF THEOLOGICAL REFLECTION WITH YOUTH: USING THE WOW METHOD

Youth ministry produces many "Wow!" moments in which teenagers are caught off guard, surprised, challenged, or overwhelmed by the experiences or people they encounter. Wow moments can be fruitful for introducing youth to the art of theological reflection. Service projects and mission trips seem to be especially prone to supplying these moments when teenagers come face-to-face with people whose lives and circumstances are drastically different from their own. Consequently, their conceptions of people, the world, or God can be upended.

"Wow!" represents the universal human reaction of awe, surprise, and bewilderment that we feel when our view of people or the world is challenged or altered. In fact, almost every language has an equivalent natural interjection that speakers use when they are left without words. When a magician disappears, a rocket defies gravity, or a news broadcaster interrupts programming with breaking news, we utter a "Wow!" Additionally, anytime we sense the holy breaking into our lives, we're prone to utter, "Wow!" Unfortunately, while youth ministry often provokes wow moments, we often are not well equipped to help youth unpack the meaning of these moments. It's not uncommon to name them—around the campfire, at the altar, or on the last night of a mission trip—but after we've helped youth name them, we may be at a loss of what to do next. In our failure to unpack the wow moments of young people's lives, we miss a ripe opportunity for theological reflection.

Theological Reflection Is An Art

What is theological reflection? It's a matter of drawing together and using our experiences, reading of Scripture, and Christian tradition to discern God's action in the world and our proper response. It's an opportunity to put our beliefs about God in dialogue with our actions and perspectives on the world, and it can be difficult.

Theological reflection is an art, and so is leading youth in theological reflection. It requires some skill and a lot of practice, but it yields incredible rewards because it takes seriously the wow moments of teenagers' lives as thin places where the Holy Spirit meets us if we will only take time to investigate them.

As with any art, there is a method to the madness. The purpose of the Wow Theological Reflection Method (WTRM) is to help youth workers lead teenagers into the art of theological reflection by providing structure to the reflection process. The WTRM is patterned on the consensus model of practical theology described in *Practical Theology: An Introduction* by Richard Osmer (Eerdmans, 2008). The WTRM attempts to operationalize the four moments of practical theology for everyday encounters so that youth and adults are guided through the process of thinking theologically about meaningful experiences in their lives.

1. The first mode of practical theology is observation or a descriptive moment in which we ask the question, "What is happening?" or "What happened?" In this moment we tell the story of our experience in rich detail. There's a particular power in telling the story of an experience that has impacted us—even if we don't yet know why we're touched by it.

2. The second moment of practical theology asks the question, "Why is this happening?" and we seek to draw on theories of the arts, sciences, or culture to better understand and explain why the encounter happened.

3. The third moment of practical theology is the normative-theological moment in which we ask the question, "What should be happening?" We draw in theological concepts, beliefs, and ideas to move beyond what happened (or what is happening) to imagine what should be happening based upon our understanding of the will and nature of God.

4. The final moment of the practical theological process is a matter of moving back toward the real world and asking, "What, in light of all this, should we do?" If we go through the practical theological process and it doesn't point us toward renewed or revised action, then we haven't done it correctly.

Too often we stop at celebrating teenagers' descriptions of wow moments, rather than engaging them in all four moments of the process. We're content with teenagers describing what happened, and fail to help them understand why it happened, what should have happened, or how they can act as a result. By failing to explore teens' wow moments, we miss opportunities for developing adolescent faith.

Practicing the Wow Method

The WTRM involves posing a series of questions that leads a group through the four moments of practical theology. Skilled leaders will not ask every question provided here but will hone in on dialoguing with teens around the questions most pertinent to the matter at hand. Deciding which questions to ask (and to avoid) takes practice and is what makes leading theological reflection an art. Ultimately, asking the right questions is less important than avoiding another pitfall: the tendency to provide all the answers. Your role as a facilitator in theological reflection is not to provide answers but to prod youth to think and reflect for themselves. In doing so they will grow in their understanding and ability to articulate their beliefs and use theological language.

The WTRM is described on the following pages as it would be used in a mission trip or service-project setting:

Step 1: Telling the Wow Story
A. Allow time for participants to write about their "wow" moment for the day: What was the conversation, incident, or person you encountered that was meaningful, shocking, sobering, poignant, and that you don't want to forget?

B. Allow someone to share a story of something or someone encountered today that made the person go "wow." If multiple people experienced the same or similar events, allow each person to briefly share.

C. What is the core element or moment in the wow story?

While everyone should write a story in Part A, it is best in group settings to choose one story/event for the group to reflect upon together. This means some will not have personally experienced the event being described. That's OK. It's still possible for everyone to participate in the reflection process. However, allowing students to tell the story richly will enhance everyone's experience in the latter stages of the reflection process.

Step 2: Why That Moment
Start this step by focusing on the core element or moment students identified as the "wow" in their story. It's very likely something about that particular moment or aspect of the story either challenged or confirmed their (and their peers') beliefs, opinions, or assumptions. The purpose of this step is to draw that out.

Here are some questions we might use to explore that:

1. What, if anything, surprised you? What beliefs about our world, or opinions about people, surprised you?

2. What emotions did that wow moment make you feel? Why do you think you felt that way?

3. What beliefs did you have about the people involved in the story before the wow moment? after?

4. What's wrong/right, fair/unfair, destructive/healing about the lives of people in the story?

Move on from this step when students are able to articulate what about the story surprised, challenged, or disoriented them.

Step 3: What Culture Says

What might the "average Joe" on the street (or your friends or others you know) say about . . .

the people involved in your story?
the situation that happened?
the reason "this part of the world" is the way it is?
the reason "these people" are the way they are?
what should be done about situations and people like this?
you and your actions?

Move on from this step when students begin to recognize how their experiences compare and contrast to what our culture expects—and what they might have expected prior to their encounter.

Step 4: A God View on the Wow

For each of these questions, state *why* you believe this might be God's perspective.

• What might be God's view of the people involved?
• What in the situation might make God angry? smile?
• What in the situation might make God sad or sorrowful?
• On what/whom might God have judgment in the story?

- On what/whom might God show compassion?
- What do you believe Christ would have done or said if he were in the story?
- How was God's love experienced (or not) by people in the story?
- What truth might God want to speak into the story?
- Can you discern God's work in the story?

Move on from this step when students start to recognize how God's view on the situation compares and contrasts with that of the culture and of participants before encountering the wow moment.

Step 5: Aligning With God

Now that students have a better understanding of how God might view the situation of the wow story, take time to consider how the group should revise and rethink its actions in the future:

- Where in the story was there opportunity to offer expressions of God's grace, love, judgment, compassion, or mercy?
- How might God want you to live or act differently?
- In what ways do you have a new perspective on people and events in the story?
- How were you changed by the wow or by the reflection?
- How might we act as agents of God's kingdom in future similar situations?

. . . .

As usual, Jeremy was skeptical by the time he finished reading the article, but he decided to give the Wow Method a shot. That evening he opened again by asking students to share highs and lows, prefacing it a bit differently: "What was your high, what was your low, and what made you go wow today?"

Several teenagers asked what is a "wow"? "As in something that surprised you, caught you off guard, made you happy, or made you angry. You know, something that made you go wow," Jeremy explained. "And I'm talking about an incident during your work and at the mission sites, not off-site breaks."

"So not something that happened at the coffee shop?" Ricardo asked with a bit of sarcasm, as a few students chuckled.

"Actually, let's *do* talk about what happened at the coffee shop," Jeremy said. Since the group was aware of the incident, he skipped the first step of WTRM and moved directly to the second step. "I'm curious, Ricardo, why did the moment they refused to sell you a drink for the homeless man stick out to you?"

"Because it was so unfair," Ricardo shot back.

"So? Why does it matter if it's unfair?" Jeremy asked, playing devil's advocate. "You still got your drink and even saved some money."

Ricardo was upset with Jeremy's feigned dismissal of the homeless man's needs and countered: "He's a person just like you and me. Just because he doesn't have money doesn't mean he's worthless. And by the way, he has a name and it's Peter."

Jeremy realized he was getting somewhere. He moved into the third step, asking others: "So, what do you think the average person on the street would think about Peter and others who are homeless?"

Several different teens called out: "They're bums and always asking for a handout"; "they're mean or dangerous"; "they're bad for business and drive off paying customers." After a few more responses, Jeremy said: "That perception explains the barista's hesitancy to sell the orange juice, doesn't it? What do you think the average person would say about Ricardo trying to buy juice for Peter or that we weren't allowed to buy the juice?"

"I think most people would think it's strange, and I think the average person might do exactly what the barista did," said Sondra.

Jeremy rode the momentum and moved into the fourth step: "What do you think might be God's view of Peter?" Jeremy queried.

"He's a child of God, just like us," Brooke offered in a quiet voice.

"How do you know that, Brooke?" Jeremy pushed. "Tell me who created Peter and who created you—and what might that have to do with God's view?"

"Um, God created Peter, and God created me," Brooke said slowly. Then the light bulb clicked on and she said quickly, "We're both created by God and we're no different. Like parents love all their children, so God loves all God's children."

"Excellent," said Jeremy. "Now, here's a question for someone else: What in this situation might make God angry?"

"The barista would make God angry," Ricardo blurted out loudly.

"I didn't ask who, but *what*," said Jeremy. "*What* might make God angry? How would you characterize what the barista did?"

Ricardo was frustrated and said, "Treating people as less than, stereotyping people, treating them unfairly because they're homeless or poor, or because of their ethnicity. My parents are from Mexico, and they've put up with so much stuff—and me too. People treat me less than because I'm brown, and it makes me angry. I'm sure it makes God angry too; it's just like what happened to Peter. I deserve respect because I'm a child of God, too. And so is Peter."

Jeremy stood still for a moment, acknowledging how the conversation had drawn out so much passion and so much hurt and respecting all that had been shared. Then he asked one last question: "How might God want us to live or act differently in light of what happened at the coffee shop—and not just with people who are homeless but with all God's children?" A few hands pierced the air and the conversation took off. *Wow*, Jeremy thought, *maybe the wow method works!*

@cymt
CENTER FOR
YOUTH MINISTRY TRAINING

EQUIPPING **YOUTH MINISTERS**
CULTIVATING **YOUTH MINISTRY**

FULFILL YOUR CALL TO YOUTH MINISTRY
THROUGH THE CYMT GRADUATE RESIDENCY

The Graduate Residency in Youth Ministry is unique to the Center for Youth Ministry Training. CYMT creates a whole-person learning environment by nurturing residents academically in the classroom, vocationally in the local church, and emotionally through personal coaching and peer interaction.

Graduate residents gain experience in a 3-year supervised practicum by being placed in a local church while earning a Master of Arts in Youth Ministry through one of our partner seminaries, Memphis Theological Seminary or Austin Presbyterian Theological Seminary. Residents are placed at a partner church within a four-hour radius of Memphis, TN or Austin, TX.

RESIDENTS RECEIVE
- Full scholarship for tuition, books, and housing
- Masters degree from accredited seminary
- A job as a youth minister in a local church
- $1,000 per month stipend

CORE COMPONENTS

COHORT
Residents are part of a dynamic, group-learning community that provides encouragement and support as they walk through ministry together.

COACHING
Residents and churches receive one-on-one coaching from a youth ministry veteran to help master and apply critical skills.

CLASSROOM
In retreat-style, four times per semester, residents will be challenged to think theologically about ministry and empowered to create ministry programs that evoke deep, life-changing Christian faith.

CHURCH
Residents get hands-on experience in a local church where they serve 25 hours weekly as a youth minister.

CARE
Residents receive pastoral care and encouragement, empowering them to seek wholeness in their life.

The Center for Youth Ministry Training is a 501(c)(3) nonprofit organization that exists to equip youth ministers and churches to develop theologically informed and practically effective youth ministries.

LEARN MORE ABOUT OUR GRADUATE RESIDENCY AND OTHER CYMT RESOURCES AT WWW.CYMT.ORG

NOTES

CPSIA information can be obtained
at www.ICGtesting.com
Printed in the USA
LVOW03s0118310817
547015LV00010B/13/P